John B. Gough.

THE
AUTOBIOGRAPHY
OF
JOHN B. GOUGH,

WITH

A CONTINUATION OF HIS LIFE TO THE PRESENT TIME.

'Raging drink! thou 'lt not enslave me;
Sparkling bowl! thou now art dim;
Angel Temperance stooped to save me
From the death within thy brim.'

WILLIAM B. TAPPAN.

LONDON:
WILLIAM TWEEDIE, 337, STRAND.

1855.

DEDICATION.

TO JESSE W. GOODRICH,
Of Worcester,

WHOSE KINDNESS CHEERED AND SUPPORTED ME

'When days were dark and friends were few;'

AND TO

MOSES GRANT,
Of Boston,

OF WHOM IT MAY WITH TRUTH BE SAID, THAT

'To relieve the wretched is his pride,'

THIS NARRATIVE OF ONE,

WHO WILL EVER, WITH AFFECTIONATE GRATITUDE, REMEMBER

THEM BOTH,

IS INSCRIBED.

AUTOBIOGRAPHY.

BY JOHN B. GOUGH.

PART FIRST.

It may be asked by many individuals, whose eyes will fall on these pages, why I have thought it requisite to add one to the already numerous autobiographies extant? I answer, that justice to myself, in some measure, demands an explicit statement of the principal incidents in an hitherto eventful life; those incidents, or, at least, many of them, having, in frequent instances, been erroneously described by the press generally. Besides this, many who have heard my verbal narrations, have intimated a desire to become more fully acquainted with a career, which, although it has extended but little beyond a quarter of a century, has been fruitful of adventure. To gratify others, rather than myself, has been my object in reducing to a permanent form my somewhat eventful history. I make no pretensions to literary merit, and trust this candid avowal will disarm criticism. Mine is, indeed, a 'short and simple annal of the poor;' and if the perusal of these pages should cheer some fainting wanderer on the world's highway, and lead him far from the haunts of evil, by the still waters of temperance, my labor will have been well repaid. Truth constitutes the merit of my tale, if it possess any merit; and most of us know that real life often furnishes stranger stories than romance ever dreamed of; and that facts are frequently more startling than fiction.

I was born on the twenty-second of August, 1817, at a romantic little watering-place, named Sandgate, in the county of Kent, England. My father had been a soldier in the fortieth and fifty-second regiment of foot, and was in the enjoyment of a pension of £20 per annum, having frequently fought during the Peninsular war, and been wounded in the neck. I remember as well as if it had been but yesterday, how he would go through military exercises with me, my mimic weapon being a broom, and my martial equipments some of his faded trappings. I was not destined, however, to see how fields were won. With what intense interest have I often listened to his descriptions of battle-fields, and how have I shuddered at contemplating the dreadful scenes which he so graphically portrayed. He was present at the memorable battle of Corunna, and witnessed its hero, Sir John Moore, carried from that fatal field. 'Here,' he would say, 'was such a regiment,—there such a battalion; in this situation was the enemy,—and yonder was the position of the general and his staff.' And then he would go on to describe the death of the hero,—his looks, and his burial near the ramparts, until my young heart would leap with excitement. Apart from such attractions as these, my father possessed few for a child. His military habits had become as a second nature with him. Stern discipline had been taught him in a severe school, and it being impossible for him to cast off old associations, he was not calculated to win the deep affections of a child, although, in every respect, he deserved and possessed my love. He received his discharge from the army in the year 1823.

My mother's character was cast in a gentler mould. Her heart was a fountain, whence the pure waters of affection never ceased to flow. Her very being seemed twined with mine, and ardently did I return her love. For the long space of twenty years she had occupied the then prominent position of schoolmistress in the village, and frequently planted the first principles of knowledge in the minds of children, whose parents had, years before, been benefited by her early instructions. And well qualified by nature and acquirements was she for the interesting but humble office she filled, if a kindly heart and a well-stored mind be the requisites. Of course, I received my first lessons at home; but as I advanced in years, it became advisable that I should be sent to a school, and to one I was accordingly sent. There was a free school in the village, but my father possessed too much independence to allow him to send me to a charity school, and, though he could ill afford it, paid a weekly sum for my instruction at the seminary of Mr. Davis, of Folkstone. I progressed rapidly in my limited education, and became a teacher in the school; two classes, as was the custom, were placed under my care; the children of one of them I initiated into the art and mystery of spelling words of two syllables, and taught the Rule of Three to a class more advanced.

As most boys will, I sometimes got into petty scrapes, and once narrowly escaped a serious disgrace. I occasionally gave the reins to a temper which was naturally passionate, and on a certain occasion, when the order of 'Teachers to your classes' was given, I exclaimed, 'I wish the classes were at the devil!' One of the boys reported my remark to the master, saying, 'Please, sir, I heard him.' He called me to him. I denied that I had uttered such words; but one boy, and another, and another asserting that

I did, with 'Please, sir, I heard him, too,' my falsehood was discovered. I then could deny no longer; and my master sternly ordered me, when the school closed, to take my slate and books home with me, and never return to the school. I sat down moodily in my place, pondering on what had occurred, and revolving within my mind what course I should pursue; for I justly dreaded my father's anger, and felt convinced that he would not pass my offence by lightly. After mature consideration, I went to my master, admitted my fault, reasoned with him, and stated how much I feared my father's anger, should I be discharged from the school. Nor were my entreaties without the desired effect; for the good man relented, and I was pardoned, my father never knowing any thing of the matter.

I was now about eight years of age, and having a keen taste for the beauties of nature, was often to be found roaming on Sandgate beach, gazing with wonder on the great deep, and, as I listened to its everlasting moan, little dreaming that three thousand miles beyond was a land in which my lot would one day be cast. There was an old castle, too, in the vicinity, which had been built years ago, — ages to my boyish mind, — by Henry the Eighth. I became a great favorite of the keeper of this ancient place, and having acquired some knowledge of the history of the bluff king Hal, I used to wander through the desolate courtyards where the rank grass grew; sit in deserted, windowless chambers, where the bat nestled and the owl screamed, or gaze from turret and battlement on the surrounding scenery. And I would in fancy people the place with its old inhabitants, and see plumed cavaliers and ruffled dames pacing the corridors or surrounding the groaning board. Katherine of Arragon, and Ann Boleyn, with Henry's other wives, flitted by me. I lived, as it were, in the past; and thus, almost unconsciously, my imagination was cultured, and my mind imbued with a love of history and poetry.

My father belonged to the Methodist persuasion, and my mother was a Baptist, but the differences in doctrine existing between them never affected their happiness. As all in such cases should do, they agreed to differ. Among other circumstances connected with this period of my life, I well remember one which much impressed me. The venerable and devoted William Wilberforce resided, during a few of the summer months, at Sandgate, for the benefit of his health. I had heard much of the great philanthropist, and was not a little delighted when my father took me to his lodgings, where a prayer-meeting was held. How it was, I know not, but I attracted Mr. Wilberforce's attention. He patted me on my head, said many kind things, and expressed wishes for my welfare. He also presented me with a book, and wrote with his own hand my name on the fly-leaf. Having acquired some reputation as a good reader, he requested me to read to him. I did so, and he expressed himself as much pleased. The book presented to me, I long since lost, but never shall I forget the kindly words of the venerable giver.

I have remarked, that I was considered to be a good reader. Often, whilst I have been sitting reading to my mother, as she sat working by our cottage-door, which faced the sea, have strangers stayed to listen, attracted by my proficiency in this art. There was a library in the village, kept by Mr Purday, and to this place many of the visitors at our watering-place resorted, to learn the news. Very frequently I was sent for to read to ladies and gentlemen; and the schoolmistress's son became a general purveyor of the gossip of the day, in return for which I was rewarded pretty liberally. On one occasion, a gentleman, to whom I had read some portions of a newspaper, was so pleased, that he took me to the library, fronting the reading-room, in the same building, and asked me what book I would like to take. Showing me a volume which contained hieroglyphical pictures, and a common prayer-book, he offered me either I might choose. Now, with all the love of a lad for pictures, I ardently desired the hieroglyphical designs, but, thinking I should be considered more favorably of if I decided on accepting the prayer-book, I chose, much against my will, the latter. My choice was applauded; and a bright half crown into the bargain, consoled me for the self-mortification my vanity had imposed.

About this time I experienced a very narrow escape from death. I went to school, at Folkstone, and was returning from that place, one day, accompanied by some other boys, playing at wagon and horses, four boys personating quadrupeds, which I was driving at rather a rapid rate. It happened that a man, who was engaged in digging a trench by the side of the road, did not perceive the four lads I was driving, they having stooped as they passed; he threw up a spadeful of clay, for the purpose of tossing it to some little distance, and the sharp edge of the implement was driven with great force against my head. I instantly sunk down insensible and deluged with blood. I was carried home by the boys, who in reality became animals of burden, still unconscious, to my terrified parents, and for days my life was despaired of. Even when recovery seemed probable, few hopes of my returning reason were entertained, although, by the providence of God, I recovered; yet, to this day, I feel the effects of that blow. When excited in speaking, I am frequently compelled to press my hands on my head, to ease the pricking and darting sensation I experience; and never, I suppose, shall I be entirely free from inconvenience from this source. My father had a tender heart, notwithstanding his habitual sternness, and he never reverted to this circumstance in after days without tears.

During my father's absence in the wars, my mother's circumstances were very straitened, although, in addition to school-keeping, she worked industriously at making a kind of lace, then very fashionable, and in the manufacture of which article she greatly excelled. On one occasion, when our necessities absolutely required extra exertion, she took her basket of work, and travelled eight and a half weary miles, to the town of Dover. Arrived there, foot-sore and heart-weary, she threaded the streets and lanes with her lace, seeking for customers, but not one did she find; and, after reluctantly abandoning the pursuit, she once more turned her face towards her home — a home desolate indeed. Painful, bitterly painful, were my mother's reflections as she drew near her door, and when she rested her dreadfully tired frame, she had nothing in the house with which to recruit her strength. During her absence, a gentleman had sent for me to the Library, and was so pleased with my reading, that he made me a present of five shillings; and Mr. Purday, in addition, gave me sixpence. O! how rich I was. Never had I possessed so vast an amount of money before, and all imaginable modes of spending it flitted before my fancy. I went to play with some other boys until my mother's return from Dover; and, soon afterwards, on entering our house, I found her sitting in her chair, bathed in tears. I asked her what was the matter? when she drew me close to her, and looking in my face, with a mournful expression which I shall never forget, informed me that all her weary journey had been fruitless — she had sold nothing. O! with what joy I drew the crown-piece and the sixpence from my pocket, and placed them in her hand; and with what delightful feelings we knelt down, whilst she poured out her heart in thankfulness to God, for the relief so seasonably provided. My mother gave me a halfpenny for myself, and I felt far happier then than I did when I received the shining silver crown-piece: it was *all* my own, to do as I liked with — to keep or spend. What an inestimable privilege! I can, in all sincerity, say, that never have I received money since then, which has afforded me such solid satisfaction; and some of my most pleasant reminiscences are circumstances connected with that boyish incident.

I ought, before this, to have mentioned that I had a sister, two years younger than myself, of whom I thought a great deal. She was my chief playmate. I used to frequently personate a clergyman, being then very fond of imitation; and having rigged up a chair into something as much resembling a pulpit as possible, I would secure her services in the way of dressing up rag dolls, which constituted my congregation, for whose especial benefit I used to pour forth my mimic oratory, very much to my own amusement, if not to the edification of my dumb friends, who sat stiff and starched, perfect patterns of propriety. Then, as a diversion, I manufactured, from an old bottomless chair, a very respectable Punch and Judy box; and many a laugh have I raised among my young companions by my performances in this line. My puppets were of home manufacture, but they passed muster well enough, especially with the boys and girls, who had never been fortunate enough to have seen the genuine personifications of these remarkable characters.

About this time, my father returned home, and soon afterwards entered the service of the Rev. J. D. Glennie, a clergyman of the Church of England, and chaplain to Lord

Darnley; and here I cannot but pay a passing tribute of respect to this pious and kind-hearted man, who always treated me with much consideration. His wife sent for me, and presented me with 'Doddridge's Rise and Progress of Religion in the Soul,' 'The Economy of Human Life,' and 'Todd's Lectures to the Young;' works which shortly afterwards I perused at sea, when voyaging to America, they having been given to me the day before I left Sandgate.

A very important change in my fortunes now occurred. I was 12 years of age; and my father, foreseeing the difficulty of procuring me a trade, made an agreement with a family of our village, who were about emigrating to America, that they, in consideration of the sum of ten guineas, paid by him, should take me with them, teach me a trade, and provide for me until I was 21 years of age. After much hesitation, my mother, from a sense of duty, yielded to this arrangement. I, boy like, felt in high glee, at the prospects before me. My little arrangements having been completed, on the 4th of June, 1829, I took a last view of my native village. The evening I was about to depart, a neighbor invited me to take tea at his house, which I did. My mother remarked to me afterwards: 'I wish you had taken tea with your mother, John;' and this little circumstance was a source of much pain to me in after years. The parting with my beloved parents was bitter. My poor mother folded me to her bosom, then she would hold me off at arm's length, and gaze fondly on my face, through her tearful eyes, reading, only as a mother could, the book of futurity for me. She hung up, on the accustomed peg, my old cap and jacket, and my school-bag, and there they remained until, years after, she quitted the house. At length the parting words were spoken, and I quitted the home of my childhood, perhaps forever.

A touching scene it was, as I went through the village towards the coach-office that evening. As I passed through the streets, many a kind hand waved a farewell, and not a few familiar voices sounded out a hearty 'God bless you.' There was one old dame, of whom I had frequently bought sweetmeats at her green grocery, named familiarly Granny Hogben; she called me into her shop, and loaded me with good wishes, bulls' eyes, cakes, and candies, although, poor affectionate soul, she could ill afford it. The inn was reached, and, in company with another lad, who was going out with our family to meet a relative, I mounted the roof of the London night coach, and was quitting the village, when, on turning round to take a last look at it, I saw a crouching female form, by a low wall, near the bathing-machines. My heart told me at once that it was my mother, who had taken advantage of half an hour's delay, at the inn door, to proceed a little distance, in order to have one more glance at her departing child. I never felt I was loved so much, as I did from that time. When we arrived at Ashford, we were placed inside the vehicle. Amongst many things which impressed me on my journey, was the circumstance of a poor, shivering woman begging alms at the coach door, at midnight, for whom I keenly felt. At Footscray, I again was placed outside the coach. On arriving near the metropolis, objects of interest increased every moment, and, when fairly in the great city, of which I had heard so much, I was almost bewildered with the crowds, and the multiplicity of attractive objects. A fight between two bellicose individuals was almost my first town entertainment

Whilst I remained in London, I saw some of the great gratuitous attractions, such as St. Paul's, the Tower, the Royal Exchange, the Mansion House, and the Monument, to the summit of which I ascended, and surveyed from thence the 'mighty mass of brick, and smoke, and shipping.' On the 10th day of June, every thing being arranged, I sailed from the Thames, in the ship Helen. Passing Dover, we arrived off Sandgate, on Sunday, when it fell a dead calm, and the ship's anchors were dropped. I afforded some amusement to those around me, by the eagerness with which I seized a telescope, and the certainty with which I averred that I saw my old home. During that day, boat after boat came off to us from the shore, and friends of the family I was with paid them visits, but I was unnoticed — *my* relatives did not come. After long and wearily watching, I at last saw a man, standing up in a boat, with a white band round his hat. 'That's him! that's my father!' I shouted. He soon got on deck, and almost smothered me with his kisses, from which I somewhat shrank, as his beard made very decided impressions on my smooth skin. I heard that my mother and sister had gone to a place of worship, at some distance from Sandgate, which I regretted much. When evening came on, our visitors from the shore repaired to their boats, which, when a few yards from the ship, formed in a half circle. Our friends stood up in them, and, o'er the calm waters sounded our blended voices, as we sang : —

> 'Blest be the dear uniting love,
> Which will not let us part;
> Our bodies may far hence remove,
> We still are one in heart.'

Boat after boat then vanished in the gloomy distance, and I went to my bed. About midnight, I heard my name called, and going on deck, I there found my beloved mother and sister, who, hearing, on their return home, that I was in the offing, had paid half a guinea (money hardly earned, and with difficulty procured, but readily and cheerfully expended) to a boatman, to row them to the ship. They spent an hour (O, how short it seemed!) with me, and then departed, with many tears. Having strained my eyes, until their boat was no longer discernible, I went back to my bed, to sob away the rest of the morning. I felt this to be my first real sorrow. Grief, however, will wear itself out; and, having slept somewhat, when I awoke in the morning, a breeze having sprung up, we were far out at sea. I never experienced any sea-sickness; and, had my expectations with respect to the family I was with been realized, I should have been comparatively happy. Occasionally, on looking over my little stock of worldly goods, I would find little billets, or papers, containing texts of Scripture, pinned to the different articles. In my Bible, texts of Scripture were marked for me to commit to memory; amongst them, I remember, were the 2d, 3d, 4th, and 5th chapters of Proverbs. As we voyaged on, I soon began to feel a difference in my new situation; and often did I bitterly contrast the treatment I received, with that to which I had been accustomed at home. I wished myself back again; but the die was cast, and so I put up with disagreeables as well as I could. On the morning of the 3d of August, fifty-four days from the time of sailing, we arrived off Sandy Hook; and, O how I longed, as we sailed up the Narrows, to be on deck, and survey the scenery of the New World! I was not permitted to do this; for, whilst I could hear the shouts of delighted surprise which burst from the lips of the passengers who crowded the vessel's sides, I was confined below, occupied in blacking the boots and shoes of the family, in order that that they might be landed 'sound, and in good order.' We made the land at three in the morning, and were moored at the wharf, in New York, at three in the afternoon, rather an unusual thing, as ships are generally detained some time at Staten Island.

I had got so tired of biscuit,* that I most ardently longed for some 'soft Tommy,' and was already munching it in imagination, when my guardians went on shore, leaving me behind. I had anticipated purchasing some dainties immediately, for, having received a little money for a cabbage-net I had made on board, I possessed the requisite funds. My capital was, however, not so large as it might have been, for I had, like other capitalists, negotiated a loan with the black cook, to whom I advanced an English crown. The principal and interest, to this day, remain unpaid, not an uncommon occurrence, I have been since told, in regard to foreign loans. To return. I was left on board all night, as my acquaintances did not return; and, during their absence, I sought for amusement in gazing from the vessel on the crowded wharfs. I well remember my surprise, at seeing a boy, about my own age, inserting a plug of tobacco in his mouth; but I soon became accustomed to such things as these, and many, too, of a far stranger nature

---

* I would here state, that the family I travelled with had provided a quantity of fine white pilot bread for the voyage. I suppose I at first ate very heartily, and that fears were entertained of my diminishing the stock; for when we arrived at Portsmouth, the head of the family went on shore, and brought back with him a bag of the most suspicious-looking biscuit I ever laid eyes on. On this I was exclusively fed during the remainder of the voyage. To do Mr. —— justice, I do not think *he* **was** altogether to blame in this matter, for I believe him to have been naturally a kind-hearted man; but it is not always that husbands can do exactly as they please in this world.

B

When I *did* get an opportunity, I laid in a good stock of bread; and having stayed about two months in York City, during which time I often strolled about the streets, we started for Western New York. I was greatly delighted with the scenery on the Hudson river, which far surpassed any I had ever before witnessed. We went to a farm in Oneida county, where I remained two years, during which period I was never sent to either a Sabbath or day school. I felt this much, as I had an ardent desire to acquire knowledge; and, tiring of so unprofitable a life, and perceiving, also, that no chance existed of my being taught a trade, I sold a knife for the purpose of paying the postage of a letter to my father, in which I asked his permission to go to New York, and learn a trade. I sent off this letter clandestinely, because, hitherto, all my letters home had been perused by my guardians before they were despatched, and I did not wish their interference in this matter. In due course, I received a reply to my letter. My father said that as I was old enough now to judge for myself, I might act according to the dictates of my own judgment. Glad enough was I to have my fate in my own hands, as it were, and on the 12th of December, 1831, I quitted Oneida county for New York city. It may easily be imagined, that I left my situation with but very little regret, for, although by some of the members I was treated with consideration and kindness, yet from those to whom I naturally looked for comfort and solace, I experienced treatment far different from that which my father anticipated when he intrusted me to their guardianship. In all conscientiousness, I can aver, that my situation, when I left this family, was worse than it was when I entered it. Here, I beg to make a remark, which is rendered necessary from the fact of it having been stated that I have represented the family as dissipated and drunken. Such a report never was made by me at any time, or in any place; nor did there exist foundation for such a rumor. Whisky and cider were used by the family, but not to excess, that I knew of. In pure self-defence I make this statement.*

Whilst with the family referred to, a revival of religion occurred in our neighborhood. My mind was much impressed, and I was admitted a member of the Methodist Episcopal Church. On my arrival in New York, I had half a dollar only in my pocket, and all the goods I possessed in the world were contained in a little trunk, which I carried. I stood at the foot of Courtland street, after I left the boat. Hundreds of people went by, on busy feet, heedless of me, and I felt desolate indeed. But, amidst all my lonely sorrow, the religious impressions I have just referred to, and, more especially, those which I had derived from the lips of my beloved mother, afforded some rays of consolation which glimmered through the gloom. Whilst I was standing, pondering whither I should bend my steps, a man came up to me, and asked where he should carry my trunk. Then, indeed, the strong sense of my forlornness came to me, and I scarcely ever remember to have experienced more bitterness of spirit than on that occasion. Fancy me, reader! a boy, just fourteen years of age, a stranger, in a strange city, with no one to guide him, none to advise, and not a single soul to love, or be loved by. There I was, three thousand miles distant from home and friends; a waif on life's wave, solitary in the midst of thou-

---

* I never should have referred to this subject, had not a meddlesome fellow in New York city busied himself about my affairs, impeached my veracity, and imputed to me motives which I never entertained. *Verbum, sat.*

sands, and with a heart yearning for kindly sympathy, but finding none. Whilst musing on my fortunes, all at once the following passage entered my mind, and afforded me consolation : 'Trust in the Lord, and do good; so shalt thou dwell in the land, and verily thou shalt be fed.' Shouldering my trunk, I entered the city; and, having left my load in charge of a person, I repaired to the Brown Jug, public-house, in Pearl street, in which place I remained until the Monday morning following, when I was recommended to apply to the venerable Mr. Dando, who was then the agent of the Christian Advocate and Journal. To this gentleman I told my story, after hearing which, he went with me to the Methodist book concern (then situated in Crosby street), where, after some conversation, I was engaged, to attend on the next Wednesday, as errand boy, and to learn the book-binding business ; and, for my services, to receive two dollars and twenty-five cents per week, and to board myself. Mr. Dando recommended me, as a boarder, to a Mrs. M——, in William street, at the rate of two dollars weekly; and, low as were the terms, the reader will presently agree with me in thinking, that it was far too much for the accommodation I received. To my surprise, I found, when the hour of rest approached, that I was to share a bed with an Irishman, who was lying very sick of a fever and ague. The poor fellow told me his little history; and I experienced the truth of the saying, that 'Poverty makes us acquainted with strange bed-fellows.' He had emigrated to America, been attacked with the disease I have mentioned, and now was out of money, but daily in the expectation of receiving some from his friends. My companion shivered so much, and was so restless during the night, that I was wretchedly disturbed; and, next day, I told my landlady that I could not possibly sleep in the same bed with the Irishman again. Accordingly, the next night, she made me up a wretched couch, in the same room, under the rafters. It was hard enough, and what is called a cat's-tail bed; and so wretchedly situated was it, that when I stretched my hand out, to pull up the scanty supply of bed-clothes, my fingers would encounter the half glutinous webs of spiders, a species of insect to which I have had, from childhood, and still have, an unaccountable, but deeply-rooted, antipathy. Weary as I was, from want of sleep on the preceding night, I soon fell asleep in my uneasy bed, but was awoke, in the dead of the night, by frightful groans, uttered by my sick companion. I started, and found, to my surprise, that the man was up. I was dreadfully frightened, more especially, as he informed me that he feared he was going to die. I asked him to let me call assistance; but he positively forbade it, and then went and sat on the side of the bed. O! never have I heard such agonizing exclamations, as broke from the lips of that dying man, as he called, with terrible earnestness, on Christ to save him, and on God to be merciful to him. He seemed anxious to know the hour. I told him I thought it was near morning, as the cock had crowed. After some more moaning noises, he suddenly fell back on the bed. I heard a rattling, gurgling sound, and then all was silent. I *felt* the man was dead, although I could not see him, and knew that I was alone with Death, for the first time. O! how slowly dragged on the hours until dawn; and, when the faint light struggled through a little window in the roof, and gradually brought out the walls and furniture from the gloom, there lay the dead man on his back, his mouth wide open, and his eyes glazed, but staring only as dead eyes can. With a desperate effort, I started from my bed, gathered my clothes in a bundle, dressed myself outside the room door, and roused the woman of the house. She received the intelligence with about as much composure as if Death had paid her house an expected and customary visit, and only remarked, 'Well, dear soul! he was very patient, and is gone to glory.' After the poor man's death, his expected funds arrived; but, alas! too late.

I soon afterwards went to my work, and my business was to pack up bundles of books for Cincinnati. As I was working, I fell into a train of thought respecting my desolate situation, and, as I mused, the scalding tears fell, in large drops, on the paper I was using. Into the very depths of my sorrow a kind heart looked; for, whilst I was weeping, a young lady came to me, and asked me what was the matter? Her tone of kindness, and look of sympathy, won my confidence, and I informed her of the particulars of my little history. When I had finished my tale, she said, 'Poor distressed child! you shall go home with me to-night.' I did so; and, when I arrived at her house, I saw her mother, who was engaged in frying cakes on the stove. The young girl took her mother aside into an inner room, and, presently, the latter came out, and said to me, 'Poor boy! I will be a mother to you.' These words fell like refreshing dew on my young heart; and mother and sister, indeed, did the benevolent Mrs. Egbert and her daughter prove to me. Soon after this, I joined the church in Allen street; and, after remaining with the Egberts some months, I removed, and boarded with my class-leader, Mr. Anson Willis. I afterwards boarded with a Mrs. Ketchum; but frequently wished that I had remained with Mrs. Egbert. During this period of my life, circumstances induced me to leave the church, and also my place of employment; and I became exposed to temptation, and too soon grew thoughtless of religious things. I now worked at N. and J. White's, corner of William and Pearl streets, and, as my prospects were somewhat improving, I sent for my father, mother, and sister, to join me in this country. On Saturday afternoon, in August, 1833, a small note was brought, which informed me that my mother and sister were on board the ship President, then lying in the stream. I immediately left my work, intending to go to them, and was on my way down Fulton street, when the sole of my shoe got loose, and I stepped into the bindery of Burlock and Wilbur, where I had directed my relatives to call on their arrival, to get a knife to cut it off, when I learned that my mother had called at the store, a short time before, and had left to go to William street. I turned into that thoroughfare, and saw a little woman, rapidly walking, whom I recognized as her of whom I was in search. She looked every now and then at a slip of paper which she held in her hand, and frequently glanced from it to the fronts of the houses, as if to ascertain some particular number. Much as I desired to speak to her, I thought I would try whether she would recognize me or not; so I went behind her, passed on a little way, then turned, and met her; but she did not observe who I was. I again went behind her, and exclaimed, 'Mother!' At the well-known sound she turned in a moment, and in an instant she had clasped me in her arms, and embraced me in a very maternal manner, heedless of the staring passers-by, who were very little used to have such public displays of affection got up for their amusement. I returned with my mother to the barge, in order to get her luggage, and, when there, was surprised by a great girl jumping into my arms, who was so altered from the time I saw her last, that I had some difficulty in recognizing my sister. My father did not accompany his wife and daughter, for he was loth to lose his hard-earned pension, and was in hopes to effect a commutation with the government, and receive a certain sum, in lieu of an annual payment.

At that time I was in the receipt of three dollars a week, wherewith to support myself; and, with the few articles my mother brought over, we went to housekeeping. O! how happy did I feel that evening, when my parent first made tea, in our own home. Our three cups and saucers made quite a grand show, and, in imagination, we were rich in viands, although our meal was frugal enough. Thus we lived comfortably together, nothing of note occurring, until the November following, when, owing to a want of business, and the general pressure of the times, I was dismissed from my place of work. This was a severe blow to us all, and its force was increased by my sister who was a straw-bonnet maker, also losing her employment. Our rent was a dollar and a quarter per week; but, finding it necessary to retrench in our expenditure, we gave up our two rooms, and made one answer our purpose, by dividing it into two compartments at night, by hanging up a temporary curtain. Our rent was now reduced to fifty cents a week, and all our goods and chattels were contained in the garret, which we continued to occupy until my mother's death. Things gradually grew worse and worse. Winter, in all its terrors, was coming on us, who were ill prepared for it. To add to our troubles, wood, during that season, was very high in price, and, in addition to want, we suffered dreadfully from cold. I obtained employment only at uncertain intervals, and for short periods, as errand-boy in a book-store, in Nassau street, and in a bindery; but, even with this aid, we were sorely off, and painfully pinched. Thus was the whole of that dreary winter one continued scene of privation. Our sorrows were aggravated by my poor mother's sickness, and our apparel began to grow wretchedly scanty. I remember my mother once wishing for some broth, made from mutton. Not being able to bear that she should want any thing she required, I took my best coat, and having pawned it, procured her some meat, and thus supplied her wants, so far as practicable. Often and often have I, when we were destitute of wood, and had no money to procure any, gone a mile or two into the country, and dragged home such pieces as I might find lying about the sides of the road. Food, too, was sometimes wanting; and once, seeing my mother in tears, I ascertained that we had no bread in the house. I could not bear the sight of such distress, and wandered down a street, sobbing as I went. A stranger accosted me, and asked me what was the matter? 'I'm hungry,' said I; 'and so is my mother.' 'Well,' said the stranger; 'I can't do much; but I'll get you a loaf;' and when I took this three cent piece of bread home, my mother placed the Bible on our old ricketty pine table, and, having opened it, read a portion of Scripture, and then we knelt down, thanking God for his goodness, and asking his blessing on what we were about to partake of. All these sufferings and privations my poor mother bore with Christian resignation, and never did she repine through all that dreary season.

As the spring came on, both my sister and myself got employment again, and our situation was bettered for a time. I now earned four dollars and a half a week; and was enabled to redeem my coat. A happy day was that, when I went in it with my sister to a place of worship. I would here mention, that, during all that hard winter, we received no charitable assistance from any source. Once, and only once, my mother spoke of some wood which was to be given away to the poor, at the City Hall; but I refused to allow her to apply for relief there, knowing well that she would be subjected to the insulting questions of hard-hearted officials, who took advantage of their office to insult the unfortunate children of penury. Pity it is, that kind actions cannot always be performed in a kindly spirit; but, too often, such is not the case, in this cold-hearted world. Glad to this day am I, that I prevented her from being mortified by a contumely, which I cannot bear to think she should have borne.

And now comes one of the most terrible events of my history, an event which almost bowed me to the dust. The summer of 1834 was exceedingly hot; and as our room was immediately under the roof, which had but one small window in it, the heat was almost intolerable, and my mother suffered much from this cause. On the eighth of July, a day more than usually warm, she complained of debility, but as she had before suffered from weakness, I was not apprehensive of danger, and saying I would go and bathe, asked her to provide me some rice and milk against seven or eight o'clock, when I should return. That day my spirits were unusually exuberant. I laughed and sung with my young companions, as if not a cloud was to be seen in all my sky, when one was then gathering which was shortly to burst in fatal thunder over my head. About eight o'clock I returned home, and was going up the steps, whistling as I went, when my sister met me at the threshold, and seizing me by the hand, exclaimed, '*John, mother's dead!*' What I did, what I said, I cannot remember; but they told me, afterwards, I grasped my sister's arm, laughed frantically in her face, and then for some minutes seemed stunned by the dreadful intelligence. As soon as they permitted me, I visited our garret, now a chamber of death, and there, on the floor, lay all that remained of her whom I had loved so well, and who had been a friend when all others had forsaken me. There she lay, with her face tied up with a handkerchief;—

> 'By foreign hands her aged eyes were closed;
> By foreign hands her decent limbs composed.'

O! how vividly came then to my mind, as I took her cold hand in mine and gazed earnestly in her quiet face, all her meek, enduring love, her uncomplaining spirit, her devotedness to her husband and children. All was now over; and yet, as through the livelong night I sat at her side, a solitary watcher by the dead, I felt somewhat resigned at the dispensation of Providence, and was almost thankful that she was taken from the 'evil to come.' Sorrow and suffering had been her lot through life; now she was freed from both; and loving her as I did, I found consolation in thinking that she was 'not lost, but gone before.'

I have intimated, that I sat all night watching my mother's cold remains; such was literally the fact; and none but myself and God can tell what a night of agony that was. The people of the house accommodated my sister below. When the morning dawned in my desolate chamber, I tenderly placed the passive hand by my mother's side, and wandered out into the as yet almost quiet streets. I turned my face towards the wharf, and, arrived there, sat down by the dock, gazing with melancholy thoughts upon the glancing waters. All that had passed seemed to me like a fearful dream, and with difficulty could I at certain intervals convince myself that my mother's death was a fearful reality. An hour or two passed away in this dreamy, half-delirious state of mind, and then I involuntarily proceeded slowly towards my wretched home. I had eaten nothing since the preceding afternoon, but hunger seemed like my other senses to have become torpid. On my arrival at our lodgings, I found that a coroner's inquest had been held on my mother's corpse, and a note had been left by the official, which stated that it must be interred by noon of the following day. What was I to do? I had no money, no friends, and what was perhaps worse than all, none to sympathize with myself and my sister, but the people about us, who could afford the occasional exclamation, 'poor things!' Again I wandered into the streets, without any definite object in view. I had a vague idea that my mother was dead, and must be buried, and little feeling beyond that. At times, I even forgot this sad reality. Weary and dispirited, I at last once more sought my lodgings, where my sister had been anxiously watching for me. I learned from her, that, during my absence, some persons had been and brought a pine box to the house, into which they had placed my mother's body, and taken it off in a cart, for interment. They had but just gone, she said. I told her that we must go and see mother buried; and we hastened after the vehicle, which we soon overtook.

There was no 'pomp and circumstance' about that humble funeral; but never went a mortal to the grave who had been more truly loved, and was then more sincerely lamented, than the silent traveller towards Potter's Field, the place of her interment. Only two lacerated and bleeding hearts mourned for her; but as the almost unnoticed procession passed through the streets, tears of more genuine sorrow were shed, than frequently fall when

'Some proud child of earth returns to dust.'

We soon reached the burying-ground. In the same cart with my mother was another mortal whose spirit had put on immortality. A little child's coffin lay beside that of her who had been a sorrowful pilgrim for many years, and both now were about to lie side by side in the 'narrow house.' When the infant's coffin was taken from the cart, my sister burst into tears, and the driver, a rough-looking fellow, with a kindness of manner that touched us, remarked to her, 'Poor little thing; 't is better off where 't is.' I undeceived him in his idea as to this supposed relationship of the child, and informed him that it was not a child but our mother for whom we mourned. My mother's coffin was then taken out and placed in a trench, and a little dirt was thinly sprinkled over it. So was she buried!

There was no burial-service read,—none. My mother was one of God's creatures, but she had lived—died amongst the poor. She had bequeathed no legacies to charitable institutions, and how could the church afford one of its self-denying men to pray over her pauper-grave? She had only been an affectionate wife, a devoted mother, and a poor Christian; so how could a bell toll with any propriety as she drew near to her final resting-place? No prim undertaker, who measured yards of woe on his face according to the number of hatbands and gloves ordered for the funeral, was there, and what need, then, of surpliced priest? Well, it was some comfort to me, that my poor mother's body could 'rest in hope,' without the hired services of either; and I could not help feeling and rejoicing that he who wept at the grave of Lazarus, was watching the sleeping dust of his servant. O! miserable indeed is the lot of the poor;—a weary, struggling, self-denying life, and then a solitary death and an unblessed grave!

From that great Golgotha we went forth together; and, unheeded by the bustling crowd, proceeded sadly to our now desolate chamber, where we sat down and gazed vacantly around the cheerless room. One by one the old familiar objects attracted our notice. Among other articles, a little saucepan remained on the extinguished embers in the grate, with rice and milk burned to its bottom! This was what my mother was preparing for me against my return from bathing, and the sight renewed my remembrances of her care, which it so happened was exercised for me in her latest moments. I afterwards was informed that she was found lying cold on the floor, by a young man who passed our room-door, on the way to his own, and saw her lying there. She seemed to have been engaged in splitting a piece of pine-wood with a knife, and it is supposed that, whilst stooping over it and forcing down the knife, she was seized with apoplexy, and immediately expired.

Whilst we were sadly contemplating our situation and circumstances, and calling to mind many sayings and doings of our lost mother, I began to think about our future course, and said to my sister, 'Now, Mary, what shall we do?' She remarked something, I forget what; and I, in turn, made an observation, to the effect, as well as I can remember, that we could take all our furniture on our backs! when we, both of us, broke out into a violent fit of laughter, which lasted for several minutes; and I never, either before or since, remember to have been so entirely unable to control myself. It was a strange thing to hear that hitherto silent chamber, in which, for hours, we had scarcely spoken above a whisper, echoing such unaccustomed sounds, but so it was; and I am unable to explain why, unless it be on the principle of reaction. And yet it was not the laugh of joy, but more like the fearfully hysterical mirth of saddened hearts, in which, for the time, all the feelings of youth had been imprisoned, but by one wild effort had broken forth, shouting with natural but unbidden glee.

On that Wednesday night, I could not bear to remain in the house, so I sauntered out, and passed the long hours of darkness in the streets;—to lie down I felt was impossible, so great was my weight of woe. The next day I passed wearily enough, and at night I procured a little sleep; but from the afternoon of my mother's death, not a morsel of food had passed my lips. I loathed food, and it was not until the Friday evening that I was persuaded to take any. Every thing about us so forcibly and painfully reminded us of her we had lost, that my sister and myself determined to remove from our lodgings; and, having disposed of our feather-bed and a few little matters to the woman of the house, we paid a week's board in advance at a house in Spring street. I now began to feel the effects of my night-watchings and neglect of food, and was taken so sick, that a city physician attended me for three or four days. As soon as I recovered, I inquired for my old and kind friends, the Egberts. They were in the city, and I proceeded to their house, in Suffolk street, where I was received cordially, and kindly nursed, with all the care of a mother and sister, during the weak time which followed my indisposition. My sister and I had separated, as she boarded where she worked, in the upper part of the city.

As soon as I had sufficiently recovered, I scraped together what money I could, and went on a visit to the family with whom I left England. With them I remained two months, and received many condolences on the subject of my mother's death and my lonely situation; but after, and, indeed, during this time, I could not help feeling that my absence would not be regretted, so I made preparations for quitting them. Whilst in the country, I spent a few days with Mr. Elijah Hunt, who, together with Mrs. Hunt, were extremely kind to me. As my wearing apparel was getting shabby, Mr. Hunt, in the kindest manner, provided me with a twenty-five dollar suit, trusting to my honor for repayment when it lay in my power. Never shall I forget the kindness of him and his family to me at that time. I started for New York about September, and there went to work for Mr. John Gladding, who always behaved kindly towards me. I boarded in Grand street; and about this time laid the foundation of many of my future sorrows.

I possessed a tolerably good voice, and sang pretty well, having also the faculty of imitation rather strongly developed; and, being well stocked with amusing stories, I got introduced into the society of thoughtless and dissipated young men, to whom my talents made me welcome. These companions were what is termed respectable, but they drank. I now began to attend the theatres frequently, and felt ambitious of strutting *my* hour upon the stage. By slow but sure degrees I forgot the lessons of wisdom which my mother had taught me, lost all relish for the great truths of religion, neglected my devotions, and considered an actor's situation to be the *ne plus ultra* of greatness. I well remember, in my early days, having entertained, through the influence of my mother, a horror of theatres; and once, as I walked up the Bowery, and watched the multitudes passing to and fro from the steps of the play-house there, which I had mounted for the sake of a better view of the busy scene, this passage of Scripture came to my recollection, 'The glory of the Lord shall cover the face of the earth as the waters cover the sea;' and I mentally offered up a prayer that that time might speedily arrive. Not very long afterwards, so low had I fallen and so desperately had I backslidden, that at the very door of that same theatre, which I had, five years before, wished destroyed, as a temple of sin, I stood applying for a situation as actor and comic singer! No longer did I wish a church should be built on the site of the theatre; that very place of entertainment had become at first a chosen, and now, to support excitement, an almost necessary, place of resort. I afterwards performed at the Franklin Theatre, under the assumed name of Gilbert, which my mother bore before she married, when a comic song of mine was so encored that I was encouraged to pursue the course I entered on, but I did not at that time.

During this period, I worked pretty steadily at my business, but such were my growing habits of dissipation, that, although receiving five dollars a week, I squandered every cent away, and was continually in debt. My proceedings, too, became characterized by a hitherto unfelt recklessness. One morning a young man came to me and informed me that a great fire had broken out down the street. (I had belonged to a volunteer fire-engine company, and also to a dramatic society, which held their meetings at the corner of Anthony street and Broadway, and which had greatly tended to increase my habits of irregularity.) I passed by the information lightly and selfishly, saying, 'Let it burn on, it wont hurt me.' When I had finished my breakfast, some one informed me the fire was in the neighborhood of the shop where I worked. This alarmed me; and I proceeded towards my place of business, where I arrived just in time to see the flames bursting through the workshop windows. By this disaster, although I had so little anticipated it, I lost what I could ill afford, an overcoat and some books; and worse than this, I was thrown out of employment; so that I *was* injured by the fire, which I had so confidently thought 'could not hurt me.'

Mr. Gladding, after the fire, determining to remove to Bristol, Rhode Island, and set up in business there, invited me to accompany him. I therefore left New York, and remained in his employ for about a year, during which time nothing of importance transpired. In February or March, 1837, however, Mr. Gladding failed, and as I was again obliged to seek for occupation, I proceeded to Providence, and there continued my drinking habits. I succeeded in procuring work at Mr. Brown's, in Market Row, and experienced much kindness at his hands. Here I might, and ought, to have done well, but for my unfortunate habits of dissipation, which gradually increased, and which were every day treasuring up misery for me.

It happened that, at this time, a company of actors were performing at Providence. I got acquainted with them, and being strongly advised by them to make an essay on the stage, I acceded to their wishes and followed my own inclinations with respect to the matter. It could not be expected that, connected with the stage, I could follow steadily a more sober occupation. Nor did I; for I worked only at uncertain intervals, frequently was absent for days together, and, as a necessary consequence, incurred the displeasure of my employer, who soon after discharged me from his shop, on the ground of inattention to my business, although I was acknowledged by him to be an excellent workman. I now entirely gave myself up to the stage, and gained some reputation for the manner in which I performed a low line of character. Brilliant, however, as I thought my prospects to be, I was doomed to disappointment; for, before long, the theatre came to a close, and I, in common with the other members of the company, failed to receive remuneration for my services. Thus was I again thrown on my own resources, and, with a tarnished reputation, my situation was far worse than it had hitherto been. I tried to obtain employment, but none could I obtain; and although I wished to get out of the town, I was unable to do so from want of funds. My clothes had grown shabby, and I was guiltless of wearing more than one suit. Worse than this, my appetite for strong drink was increasing, and becoming a confirmed habit — the effect of almost unlimited indulgence. I was now reduced to absolute want. My boarding-house account had assumed an unpleasant aspect, and, more than once, had I received threatening notices to quit. One night I was reduced to extremities, and so poorly was I off, that I was compelled to wander about the streets, from night until almost morning, in order to keep myself warm. In pure desperation, I repaired to one of the very lowest class of hotels, where I obtained a miserable lodging. It happened, at this time, that a person visited Providence who wanted to engage some performers for a theatre which was to open, for a short season, in Boston. To this person, whose name was Barry (and who, afterwards, was lost, with his whole stock company, whilst going to Texas), I was introduced; and he was, at the same time, informed of my necessity. Mr. Barry, with a kindness, which was well meant, said he would take me to Boston with him, on his own responsibility, and use his influence in my behalf. I left Providence, on a Sunday morning, and succeeded in getting an engagement in Boston. During this time, my sister was working at her trade in Providence. I performed low comedy parts, until the theatre closed, in 1837, when I was again deprived of pay, and once more thrown, like a football, on the world's great highway, at the mercy of every passing foot. My appearance was now shabby enough, as that of a strolling player generally is. All my little stock of money was spent as fast as I received it; and, once more, I was absolutely in want. Like many others, similarly circumstanced to myself, I experienced, in my adversity, kindness from woman. A Mrs. Fox, with whom I boarded, was quite aware of my destitute situation, and benevolently afforded me a home and subsistence until I could once more obtain work. This I at last did, at Mr. Benjamin Bradley's, and in his employ I continued until the month of January, 1838, when I was discharged. The reason assigned by Mr. Bradley, for my dismissal, was what might have been expected from a knowledge of my habits. He said I was too shabby in appearance for a shop, and it was his opinion, as well as that of others, that I drank too much. I had paid my board at Mrs. Fox's up to that time, but was now again without a cent, and was in the depths of trouble, until I accidentally heard that a person at Newburyport was in want of a binder, to whom he was willing to give six dollars a week wages. Small as was this remuneration, I need scarcely say that I eagerly accepted the offered salary, and travelling, partly by stages, and partly in cars, entered Newburyport late in the evening of the 30th of January. The next morning I commenced work in my new situation, and, for a few weeks, by a desperate effort, I managed to keep free from the intoxicating cup. I was now comparatively steady, and gave satisfaction to my employer; but this state of things, unhappily did not last long, for, I regret to say, I had a longing for society, and soon formed an acquaintance with companions who were calculated to destroy any resolutions of amendment which I had formed. I joined a fire-engine company, and, before long, I was again on the high-road of dissipation, neglecting my business, destroying my reputation, which was already damaged, and injuring my health.

Work grew slack towards the July of that year, and, as

I could not earn sufficient to support myself at my trade, I embraced another occupation, and entered into an arrangement, with the captain of a fishing-boat, to go a voyage with him down Chaleur bay. My sea experiences were somewhat severe, as will presently be seen; but as there was no rum on board, I was forced to keep sober, and that at least, saved me a considerable amount of suffering When, however, I went on shore, I made up for my forced abstinence by pottle-deep potations, and my visit to another vessel was generally accompanied by a carousal, if rum was by any means to be obtained. In consequence of what is commonly called a 'spree,' my life was, at one time, placed in considerable jeopardy. Several of our crew, with myself, had been on board a neighbouring vessel, and, on our return at night, I was, as might be expected, very drunk. The boat was rowed to the side of our craft, and I was so much intoxicated, that, unnoticed, I lay at the bottom of the boat. As customary, when the rest of the crew got on board, the hook was fastened in the bow of the boat, which was drawn up. In consequence of this, as the bow was hoisted with a jerk, I was flung violently, from where I was lying, to the stern, and the force of the blow effectually awakened me. I called out, and alarmed my companions, just in time to prevent being thrown overboard; and was soon rescued from my perilous position. It seemed that they had not noticed me in the boat when they left it, and supposed, in the dark scramble, I had got safely on board. So was my life again saved by an all-wise Providence; but I was so closely wrapped up in my garb of thoughtlessness, that I passed by the matter with little thought or thankfulness.

And yet, at this time, I did not consider myself to be what in reality I was — a drunkard. Well enough did I know, from bitter experience, that character, situations, and health, had been periled, in consequence of my love of ardent spirits. I felt, too, an aching void in my breast, and conscience frequently told me that I was on the broad road to ruin; but that I was what all men despised, and I, among them, detested, I could not bring myself to believe I would frame many excuses for myself—plead my own cause before myself, as judge and jury, until I obtained, at my own hands, a willing acquittal. O! how little does the young man dream that he is deceiving himself, though not others, whilst pursuing so fatal a course as was mine. He, as I did, abhors the name of 'drunkard,' whilst no other word so aptly and accurately defines his position.

The purpose of our voyage having been answered we prepared for our homeward sail, and were making for port when a violent storm burst over us. It was a Southeaster, and in our perilous position off Cape Sable none of us expected to weather it. For hours we expected to go to the bottom, and scarce a hope remained to cheer us, the captain having given up every thing for lost. We could discern the sea breaking violently over the Brazil rock four miles and a half off from us, and we were rapidly drifting to the coast; but in that dreadful season, strange to tell, I suffered but very little, if any thing, from alarm or anxiety. What to attribute this feeling, or rather absence of feeling to, I know not; but so it was, that owing to callousness or some other cause, I felt not the slightest fear, although some old 'Salts' were dreadfully anxious, and prayed in agonizing accents for deliverance. I sat as calmly as ever I remember to have done in my life whilst wave after wave dashed over the frail vessel, making every timber creak, and her whole frame to quiver as if with mortal agony. By the mercy of God, however, the wind

shifted to the westward, and by means of the only rag of a sail which remained to us we managed to crawl off. Next morning at daylight having discovered land we made towards it, and about noon anchored in Shelburne bay, Nova Scotia, where we remained long enough to replace a lost sail, and repair our damaged vessel. We soon set sail once more, and I arrived in Newburyport on the first Sunday in November, glad enough to be freed from my imprisonment for three and a half months in a small vessel of fifty tons burden.

Once more on land I engaged to work at my own business, and did so for some time with Mr. Tilton. Not long afterwards I entered into the matrimonial state, and commenced housekeeping, having earned money sufficient by my fishing voyage to purchase some neat furniture. In my new condition I might have done well, for I had every prospect of success, had it not been for my craving after society, which in spite of having a home of my own I still felt. Alas! forgetful of a husband's home duties I again became involved in a dissipated social network, whose fatal meshes too surely entangled me, and unfitted me for that active exertion which was now rendered doubly necessary. I continued at my work until the month of June, when business becoming slack, I again went on a fishing excursion with my wife's brother, the captain of the boat, into the Bay of Fundy. We were away this time for only six weeks, and returned in safety, without having encountered any thing worthy of note.

During my residence at Newburyport, my early serious impressions on one occasion in a measure revived, and I felt some stingings of conscience for my neglect of the Sabbath and religious observances. I recommenced attending a place of worship, and for a short time I attended the Rev. Mr. Campbell's church, by whom, as well as by several of his members, I was treated with much Christian kindness. I was often invited to Mr. Campbell's house, as well as to those of some of his hearers, and it seemed as if a favorable turning-point or crisis in my fortunes had arrived. Mr. Campbell was good enough to manifest a very great interest in my welfare, and frequently experienced a hope that I should be enabled, although late in life, to obtain an education. And this I might have acquired had not my evil genius prevented my making any efforts to obtain so desirable an end. My desire for strong liquors and company seemed to present an insuperable barrier against all improvement; and, after a few weeks, every aspiration after better things had ceased, every bud of promised comfort was crushed. Again I grieved the Spirit which had been striving with my spirit, and ere long became even more addicted to the use of the infernal draughts which had already wrought me so much woe, than at any previous period of my existence.

And now my circumstances began to be desperate indeed. In vain were all my efforts to obtain work, and at last I became so reduced, that at times I did not know, when one meal was ended, where on the face of the broad earth I should find another. Further mortification awaited me, and by slow degrees I became aware of it. The young men with whom I had associated in bar-rooms and parlors, and who wore a little better clothing than I could afford to put on, one after another began to drop my acquaintance. If I walked in the public streets I too quickly perceived the cold look, the averted eye, the half recognition.—and to a sensitive spirit, such as I possessed, such treatment was almost past endurance. To add to the mortification, caused by such treatment, it happened that those who had laughed the loudest at my songs and stories, and who had been social enough with me in the bar-room, were the very individuals who seemed most ashamed of my acquaintance. I felt that I was shunned by the respectable portion of the community also, and once, on asking a lad to accompany me in a walk, he informed me that his father had cautioned him against associating with me. This was a cutting reproof, and I felt it more deeply than words can express. And could I wonder at it? No. Although I may have used bitter words against that parent, my conscience told me that he had done no more than his duty in preventing his son being influenced by my dissipated habits. Oh! how often have I laid down and bitterly remembered many who had hailed my arrival in their company as a joyous event. Then plaudits would ring in my ears, and peals of laughter ring again in my deserted chamber; then would succeed stillness only broken by the beatings of my agonized heart, which felt that the gloss of respectability had worn off and exposed my threadbare condition. To drown these reflections I would drink, not from love of the taste of the liquor, but to become so stupefied by its fumes as to steep my sorrows in a half oblivion; and from this miserable stupor I would wake to a fuller consciousness of my situation, and again would I banish my reflections by liquor.

It has been said, that no one is ever utterly forlorn and friendless. Whether this be the case or not, it is not for me to decide. In my own case, and in what seemed my last extremity, I obtained some assistance. There resided in Newburyport a countryman of mine, named Low. He was an Englishman, and perhaps felt some interest in me as an old-countryman. Mr. Low was a warm-hearted and generous-minded man, and perceiving that I possessed some abilities, which he regretted to see thrown away, he very kindly manifested a desire to afford me assistance. He was a rum-seller, and I had spent many a shilling at his bar, so that he had frequent opportunities of becoming acquainted with my 'ways and means.' It occurred to me, that if I could get some tools, it was just possible I might get into business, and, by perseverance and sobriety, succeed in redeeming myself from the fallen state I was in, and, in some measure, at least, retrieve my fallen, ruined fortunes. Mr. Low assisted me very materially in my endeavors to regain a respectable position in society, by furnishing me with sufficient funds for procuring tools, so that I might work on my own account.

Despite of all that had occurred, my good name was not so far gone, but that I might have succeeded, by the aid of common industry and attention, in my business. I was a good workman, found no difficulty in procuring employment, and, I have not the slightest doubt, should have succeeded in my endeavors to get on in the world, but for my unhappy love of stimulating drinks, and my craving for society. I was now my own master — all restraint was removed, and, as might be expected, I did as I pleased in my own shop. I became careless, was often in the bar-room, or carousing in the parlor, when I should have been at my bindery; and, instead of spending my evenings at home, in reading or conversation, they were, almost invariably, passed in the company of the rum bottle, which became almost my sole household deity. Five months only did I remain in business, and, during that short period, I gradually sunk deeper and deeper in the scale of degradation. I was now the slave of a habit which had become completely my master, and which fastened its remorseless fangs in my very vitals. Thought was a torturing thing. When I looked back, Memory drew fearful pictures, in lines of lurid flame; and, whenever I dared anticipate the future, Hope refused to illumine my onward path. I dwelt in one awful present. Nothing to solace me — nothing to beckon me onwards to a better state. I knew, full well, that I was proceeding on a downward course, and crossing the sea of Time, as it were, on a bridge perilous as that over which Mahomet's followers are said to enter Paradise. A terrible feeling was ever present, that some evil was impending, which would soon fall on my devoted head; and I would shudder, as if the sword of Damocles, suspended by its single hair, was about to fall, and utterly destroy me.

Warnings were not wanting; but they had no voice of terror for me. I was intimately acquainted with a young man in the town, and well remember his coming to my shop one morning, and asking the loan of ninepence, with which to buy rum. I let him have the money, and the spirit was soon consumed. He begged me to lend him a second ninepence, but I refused; yet, during my temporary absence, he drank some spirit of wine, which was in a bottle in the shop, and used by me in my business. He went away, and the next I heard of him was, that he had died shortly afterwards. Such an awful circumstance as this might well have impressed me; but habitual indulgence had almost rendered me proof against salutary impressions. I was, to tell the truth, at this time, deeper in degradation than at any period, before or since, which I can remember.

My custom now was, to purchase my brandy, which, in consequence of my limited means, was of the very worst description, and keep it at the shop, where, by little and little, I drank it, and continually kept myself in a state of excitement. This course of proceeding entirely unfitted me for business, and it not unfrequently happened, when I had books to bind, that I would, instead of attending to business, keep my customers waiting, whilst in the company of dissolute companions. I drank during the whole day, to the complete ruin of my prospects in life. So entirely did I give myself up to the bottle, that those of my companions who fancied they still possessed some claims to respectability, gradually withdrew from my company. At my house, too, I used to keep a bottle of gin, which was in constant requisition. Indeed, go where I would, stimuli I must, and did, have. Such a slave was I to the bottle that I resorted to it continually, and in vain was every effort, which I occasionally made, to conquer the debasing habit. I had become a father; but God, in his mercy, removed my little one at so early an age, that I did not feel the loss as much as if it had lived longer, to engage my affections.

A circumstance now transpired, which attracted my attention, and led me to consider my situation, and whither I was hurrying. A lecture was advertised, to be delivered by the first reformed drunkard, Mr. J. J. Johnson, who visited Newburyport, and I was invited by some friends, who seemed to feel an interest, to attend, and hear what he had to say. I determined, after some consideration, to go, and hear what was to be said on the subject. The meeting was held at the Reverend Mr. Campbell's church, which was greatly crowded. I went, and heard the speaker depict, in forcible and graphic terms, the misery of the drunkard, and the awful consequences of his conduct, both as they affected himself, and those connected with him. My conscience told me that the truth was spoken by the lecturer, for what had I not suffered from intemperance? I remained only about ten minutes, and, as I left the chapel, a young man offered me the pledge to sign. I actually turned to sign it, but, at that critical moment, the appetite for strong drink, as if determined to have the mastery over me, came in all its force, and remembering, too, just then, that I had a pint of brandy at home, I deferred signing, and put off, to a 'more convenient season,' a proceeding which might have saved me so much after sorrow. I however compromised the matter with my conscience, by inwardly resolving that I would drink up what spirit I had by me, and then *think* of leaving off the use of the accursed liquid altogether.

'Think of it!' O! had I *then acted*, what misery would have been spared me in after days. One would have imagined that I had had my fill of misery, and been glad to have hailed and grasp any saving hand which might be held out. But, O! such was the dominion which rum had over me, that I was led captive by it, as at will. It had impaired every energy, and almost destroyed the desire to be better than I was. I was debased in my own eyes, and, having lost my self-respect, became a poor, abject being, scarcely worth attempting to reform. *Did* I *think* of it? O, no. I forgot the impressions made upon me by the speaker at the meeting I have alluded to. Still I madly drained the inebriating cup, and speedily my state was worse than ever. O, no, I soon ceased to think about it, for my master passion, like Aaron's rod, swallowed up every thought and feeling, opposed to it, which I possessed.

My business grew gradually worse, and, at length, my constitution became so impaired, that, even when I had the will, I did not possess the power to provide for my daily wants. My hands would, at times, tremble so, that I could not perform the finer operations of my business — the finishing and gilding. How could I letter straight with a hand burning and shaking, from the effects of a debauch! Sometimes, when it was absolutely necessary to finish off some work, I have entered the shop with a stern determination not to drink a single drop until I completed it. I have bitterly felt, that my failing was a matter of common conversation in the town, and a burning sense of shame would flush my fevered brow, at the conviction that I was scorned by the respectable portion of the community. But these feelings passed away, like the morning cloud or the early dew, and I pursued my old course.

To what shifts was I reduced, in order to conceal my habit of using intoxicating drinks! Frequently have I taken a pitcher, with a pint of new rum in it, purchased at some obscure groggery, and put about one third as much water as there was spirit in it, at the town pump, in the Market square, in order to induce persons to think that I drank water alone. This mixture I would take to my shop, and, for days and days together, it would be my only beverage. In consequence of this habit, I would frequently fall asleep, or, if awake, be in so half torpid a state, that work, or exertion of any kind, was quite out of the question; and, after an indulgence in this practice for some time, I was compelled to remain at home, from sheer inability to enter on active duty. I grew, of course, poorer and poorer, and my days dragged wearily on. At times, I almost wished that my life, and its miseries, would close.

The reader will remember, that I have before referred to my sister. She had been for some time married, and was then residing at Providence, Rhode Island. One day, I received a letter from her, in which she stated that she was severely afflicted with salt rheum, and requested my wife would visit her, for the purpose of nursing her and her infant. My wife deciding on going. I accompanied her to the cars, and then returned home. It was the first time, since our marriage, that we had ever been separated, and the house to me looked lonely and desolate. I thought I would not go to work, and a great inducement, to remain at home, existed in the shape of my enemy, West India rum, of which I had nearly a gallon in the house. Although the morning was by no means far advanced, I sat down, intending to do nothing until dinner time. I could not sit alone, without rum, and I drank, glass after glass, until I became so stupefied, that I was compelled to lie down on the bed, where I soon fell asleep. When I awoke, it was late in the afternoon, and then, as I persuaded myself, too late to make a bad day's work good. I invited a neighbor, who, like myself, was a man of intemperate habits, to spend the evening with me. He came, and we sat down to our rum, and drank together freely, until late that night, when he staggered home; and so intoxicated was I, that, in moving to go to bed, I fell over the table, broke a lamp, and lay on the floor for some time, unable to rise. At last, I managed to get to bed; but, O! I did not sleep, for the drunkard never knows the blessings of undisturbed repose. I awoke in the night, with a raging thirst. My mouth was parched, and my throat was burning; and I anxiously groped about the room, trying to find more rum, in which I sought to quench my dreadful thirst. No sooner was one draught taken, than the horrible dry feeling returned; and so I went on, swallowing repeated glassfuls of the spirit, until, at last, I had drained the very last drop which the jar contained. My appetite grew by what it fed on; and, having a little money by me, I with difficulty got up, made myself look as tidy as possible, and then went out to buy more rum, with which I returned to the house. The fact will, perhaps, seem incredible, but so it was, that I drank spirits continually, without tasting a morsel of food, for the next three days. This could not last long; a constitution of iron strength could not endure such treatment, and mine was partially broken down by previous dissipation.

I began to experience a feeling, hitherto unknown to me. After the three days drinking, to which I have just referred, I felt, one night, as I lay on my bed, an awful sense of something dreadful coming upon me. It was as if I had been partially stunned, and now, in an interval of consciousness, was about to have the fearful blow, which had prostrated me, repeated. There was a craving for sleep, sleep, blessed sleep! but my eyelids were as if they could not close. Every object around me, I beheld with startling distinctness, and my hearing became unnaturally acute. Then, to the singing and roaring in my ears, would suddenly succeed a silence, so awful, that only the stillness of the grave might be compared with it. At other times, strange voices would whisper unintelligible words, and the slightest noise would make me start, like a guilty thing. But the horrible, burning thirst was insupportable, and, to quench it, and induce sleep, I clutched, again and again, the rum-bottle, hugged my enemy, and poured the infernal fluid down my parched throat. But it was of no use — none. I could not sleep. Then I bethought me of tobacco; and, staggering from my bed to a shelf near, with great difficulty I managed to procure a pipe and some matches. I could not stand to light the latter, so I lay again on the bed, and scraped one against the wall. I began to smoke, and the narcotic leaf produced a stupefaction. I dosed a little; but, feeling a warmth on my face, I awoke, and discovered my pillow to be on fire! I had dropped a lighted match on the bed. By a desperate effort, I threw the pillow from the bed, and too exhausted to feel annoyed by the burning feathers, I sank again into a state of somnolency. How long I lay, I do not exactly know, but I was roused from my lethargy by the neighbors, who, alarmed by a smell of fire, came to my room to ascertain the cause. When they took me from my bed, the under part of the straw with which it was stuffed was smouldering, and, in a quarter of an hour more, must have burst into a flame. Had such been the case, how horrible would have been my fate, for it is more than probable that, in my half-senseless condition, I should have been suffocated, or burned to death. The fright produced by this accident, and very narrow escape, in some degree sobered me; but what I felt more than any thing else, was the exposure. Now, all would be known, and I feared my name would become, more than ever, a by-word and a reproach.

Will it be believed that I again sought refuge in rum? Scarcely had I recovered from the fright than I sent out, procured a pint of rum, and drank it all in less than half an hour? Yet so it was. And now came upon me many terrible sensations. Cramps attacked me in my limbs which racked me with agony, and my temples throbbed as if they would burst. So ill was I, that I became seriously alarmed and begged the people of the house to send for a physician. They did so, but I immediately repented having summoned him, and endeavored, but ineffectually, to get out of his way when he arrived. He saw at a glance what was the matter with me, ordered the persons about me to watch me carefully, and on no account to let me have any spirituous liquors. Every thing stimulating was rigorously denied me, and then came on the drunkard's remorseless Torturer — delirium tremens, in all its terrors, attacked me.

For three days I endured more agony than pen could describe, even were it guided by the mind of a Danté.

Who can tell the horrors of that horrible malady, aggravated as it is by the almost ever-abiding consciousness that it is self-sought. Hideous faces appeared on the walls, and on the ceiling, and on the floors; foul things crept along the bed-clothes, and glaring eyes peered into mine. I was at one time surrounded by millions of monstrous spiders, who crawled slowly; slowly over every limb, whilst the beaded drops of persperation would start to my brow, and my limbs would shiver until the bed rattled again. Strange lights would dance before my eyes, and then suddenly the very blackness of darkness would appal me by its dense gloom. All at once, whilst gazing at a frightful creation of my distempered mind, I seemed struck with sudden blindness. I knew a candle was burning in the room, but I could not see it. All was so pitchy dark. I lost the sense of feeling too, for I endeavored to grasp my arm in one hand, but consciousness was gone. I put my hand to my side, my head, but felt nothing, and still I knew my limbs and frame *were* there. And then the scene would change. I was falling — falling swiftly as an arrow far down into some terrible abyss, and so like reality was it that as I fell I could see the rocky sides of the horrible shaft, where mocking, jibing, mowing, fiendlike forms were perched; and I could feel the air rushing past me making my hair stream out by the force of the unwholesome blast. Then the paroxysm sometimes ceased for a few moments and I would sink back on my pallet drenched with perspiration, utterly exhausted, and feeling a dreadful certainty of the renewal of my torments.

By the mercy of God I survived this awful seizure; and when I rose a weak, broken-down man, and surveyed my ghastly features in a glass, I thought of my mother, and asked myself how I had obeyed the instructions I had received from her lips, and to what advantage I had turned the lessons she taught me. I remembered her countless prayers and tears, thought of what I had been but a few short months before, and contrasted my situation with what it then was. Oh! how keen were my own rebukes; and in the excitement of the moment I resolved to lead a better life, and abstain from the accursed wine-cup. For about a month, terrified by what I had suffered, I adhered to my resolution; then my wife came home, and in my joy at her return, I flung my good resolutions to the wind, and foolishly fancying that I could now restrain my appetite, which had for a whole month remained in subjection, I took a glass of brandy.

That glass aroused the slumbering demon, who would not be satisfied by so tiny a libation. Another, and another succeeded, until I was again far advanced in the career of intemperance. The night of my wife's return I went to bed intoxicated. I will not detain the reader by the particulars of my every-day life at this time; they may easily be imagined from what has already been stated. My previous bitter experience, one would think, may have operated as a warning, but none save the inebriate can tell the almost resistless strength of the temptations which assail him.

I did not, however, make quite so deep a plunge as before. My tools I had given into the hands of Mr. Gray, for whom I worked, and received at the rate of five dollars a week. My wages were paid me every night, for I was not to be trusted with much money at a time, so certain was I to spend a great portion of it in drink. As it was, I regularly got rid of one third of what I daily received for rum. I soon left Mr. Gray, under the following circumstances. There was an exhibition of the Battle of Bunker

Hill to be opened in the town, and the manager knowing that I had a good voice and sung pretty well, thought my comic singing would constitute an attraction; so he engaged me to give songs every evening, and to assist in the general business of the Diorama. In this occupation I continued about three weeks or a month, and when the exhibition closed in Newburyport, by invitation, I remained with the proprietor and proceeded with him to Lowell. As it was uncertain when I should return, the manager wishing me to travel with him, I sold off what few articles of furniture yet remained in my possession, and my wife arranged to stay, during my absence, with her sister. I stayed in the town of Lowell for the space of three months, my habits of intemperance increasing, as might be expected, for in a wandering life my outbreaks were not so much noticed as when I was residing at home. As had been the case often before, rum claimed nearly all my attention, and consequently the business I was called upon to perform was entirely neglected or carelessly attended to. On several occasions when I repaired to the place where the Diorama was exhibited, I was in such a state that I could do nothing required of me, and severe were the rebukes I received in consequence from my employer. These remarks incensed me highly, and only made me drink more, so that ere long my name and that of an incorrigible drunkard were synonymous. We next proceeded to Worcester, and there remained a fortnight. I experienced great difficulty in procuring the meagre salary which was promised me, and many privations had I to endure in consequence; my stock of wearing apparel was scanty enough, and hardly fit to appear in the street. This was in the month of October, and as the winter was drawing on fast, I miserably contemplated what my situation would be through the approaching severe season. Want and cold appeared before me in all their frightful realities, and I again resolved to abstain from the maddening influences which governed me with despotic rule.

I sent to my wife, requesting her to return, and transmitted her three dollars, for her expenses to Worcester, being the first money I had sent to her for four months, except five dollars which I received as part of the proceeds of a concert I gave at Lowell. I adhered, in a great measure, to my resolution not to become intoxicated, and had written to my wife, telling her of my determination to reform. On the day I expected her to return home, I met with an acquaintance, who asked me to stroll about with him, in order that he might see the town. We drank together; and our walk ended by my getting drunk, and forgetting the good resolutions which I had made. In the evening, when I was reeling along from the hotel towards the exhibition, I chanced to see a stage, and approached it, in order to see if my wife was there. She had arrived; and I took her with me to the hotel, where she discovered I had been drinking, and when she reminded me of the promise I had made her to abandon the destructive habit, I felt thoroughly ashamed of my weakness. I then went to the performance, and managed to get through my work. Soon after this, I quitted the service of the proprietor of the Diorama; and, putting as sober a face upon matters as I could, I applied to Messrs. Hutchinson and Crosby for employment. These gentlemen agreed to take me on trial, stating that, if they were satisfied with my work, they would engage me. My work was approved of; and, once more installed in a good situation, I had a chance of pushing my fortune.

My wife now began to exhibit symptoms of declining health, and my prospects as before were none of the brightest. I managed to keep my situation, and fancied that my intemperate habits were known only to myself, as I carefully avoided any open or flagrant violation of propriety,—but drunkenness, more than any other vice, cannot long be hidden. It seems as if the very walls whispered it; and there is scarcely an action of the drinking man which does not betray him. I did not, however, long remain cautious; for one morning, after having drank freely the evening before, I felt unable to work, and was compelled to remain at home during that day and the next. All my property, which I could by any means render available, I had disposed of, in order to procure money for purchasing drink; and the man in whose house I boarded, having watched my proceedings with a very vigilant and interested eye, became, I suppose, fearful that I should not be able to pay for my board, and informed my employers, Messrs. Hutchinson and Crosby, that I was detained at home in consequence of what is called a drunken spree. I do not think the information was given from any motive of kindness towards myself, but believe it was a selfish motive which prompted the interference.

I felt wretched enough when I proceeded to the shop to resume my work. Mr. Hutchinson was a man of great moral purity of character, but he had a strong hatred of intemperance, and looked not very lightly on my transgression. As soon as he saw me, he sternly informed me that he did not want any men in his employ who were in the habit of being the worse for liquor; and threatened me with instant dismissal, should I ever again neglect my business for the bottle. I assured him that he should not again have occasion to complain of my inebriety, and I inwardly resolved to profit by the warning I had received. Having a sick wife, and being almost utterly destitute of means, reflection would force itself upon me. I was startled at the idea of her and myself coming to want, entirely in consequence of my evil habit, and I resolved again to attempt the work of reformation.

In order to render myself less liable to temptation, and to avoid the dissipated society which I was constantly falling into at the hotel, where I lived, I left it, and engaged board at the house of a gentleman, who happened to be the president of a temperance society. Here I attempted to restrain my appetite for drink, but the struggle was terrible; so mighty a power would not be conquered without contesting every inch of his dominion; and I, trusting to my own strength, assailed it with but a feeble weapon. I felt as if I *could* not do without the draughts which I had been so long accustomed to, and yet I was ashamed to display the weakness which prompted me to indulge in them. To procure liquor, I was compelled to resort to every kind of stratagem, and the services of my inventive faculties were in constant requisition. Many a time would I steal out, when no one noticed me, and proceed, with a bottle in my pocket, to the farthest extremity of the town, where I would purchase a supply of rum, which I would take home with me. Occasionally I would procure spirit at the apothecary's shop, alleging, as an excuse, that it was required in a case of sickness; and the pint I would generally divide into three portions, one of which I took in the morning, another at noon, and the remainder I disposed of in the evening. My habits were not naturally of a deceptive character, and I always felt degraded in my own esteem, whenever I had occasion to resort to the expedients I have mentioned,— but what will not a drunkard do, in order to procure the stimulus he so ardently desires? Have it I would, and get it I did; and I always seemed to desire it the more when the difficulty of procuring it was increased.

My wardrobe, as had, indeed, been nearly always the case with me whilst I drank to excess, was now exceedingly shabby, and it was with the greatest difficulty that I could manage to procure the necessaries of life. My wife became very ill. O! how miserable I became. Some of the females who were in attendance on my wife, told me to get two quarts of rum. I procured it, and as it was in the house, and I did not anticipate serious consequences, I could not withstand the strong temptation to drink. I did drink, and so freely, that the usual effect was produced. How much I swallowed, I cannot tell, but the quantity, judging from the effects it produced, must have been considerable.

Ten long, weary days of suspense passed, at the end of which my wife and her infant both died. Then came the terribly oppressive feeling, that I was utterly alone in the world; and it seemed, almost, that I was forgotten of God, as well as abandoned by man. All the consciousness of my dreadful situation pressed heavily indeed upon me, and keenly as a sensitive mind could, did I feel the loss I had experienced. I drank, now, to dispel my gloom, or to drown it in the maddening cup; and soon was it whispered, from one to another, until the whole town became aware of it, that my wife and child were lying dead, and that I was drunk! But if ever I was cursed with the faculty of thought, in all its intensity, it was then. And this was the degraded condition of one who had been nursed on the lap of piety, and whose infant tongue had been taught to utter a prayer against being led into temptation. There, in the room where all who had loved me were lying in the unconscious slumber of death, was I gazing, with a maudlin melancholy imprinted on my features, on the dead forms of those who were flesh of my flesh and bone of my bone. During the miserable hours of darkness, I would steal from my lonely bed to the place where my dead wife and child lay, and, in agony of soul, pass my shaking hand over their cold faces, and then return to my bed, after a draught of rum, which I had obtained, and hidden under the pillow of my wretched couch. At such times, all the events of the past would return, with terrible distinctness, to my recollection, and many a time did I wish to die, for Hope had well nigh deserted me, both with respect to this world and the next. I had apostatized from those pure principles which once I embraced, and was now —

'A wandering, wretched, worn, and weary thing,
Ashamed to ask, and yet I needed help.'

I will not dwell on this painful portion of my career, but simply remark, that all the horrors, which I believe man could bear, were endured by me at that dreary time. My frame was enervated, my reputation gone; all my prospects were blighted, and misery seemed to have poured out all her vials on my devoted head. The funerals of my wife and child being over, I knew not what course to pursue. for, wherever I went, I failed not to see the slow moving finger of scorn pointed at me, and I writhed in agony, under the sense of shame which it produced. Every one looked coldly at me, and but few hesitated to sneer at my despicable condition. What *had* I done to deserve all this torturing treatment? I was naturally of a kind and humane disposition, and would turn aside from an unwillingness to hurt a worm: frequently have I reasoned with boys who inflicted cruelty on dumb animals. I would have hugged the dog that licked my hand, and taken to my bosom, even a reptile, if I thought it loved me. What *had* I done, to make me so shunned and execrated by my kind? Conscience gave me back an answer — I drank! and in those two words lay the whole secret of my miserable condition.

It was not to be expected that, whilst I persisted in my drinking habits, I should attend to my work. My employers perceived that I neglected their interests, as well as my own, and I was informed by them that they were no longer in need of my services. What was I to do? I had incurred some debts, which I wished to discharge, and I expressed a desire to that effect. After some hesitation, I was reëngaged, on the understanding that I should receive not one farthing of money for my labors, lest it should be spent in liquor. My employers said they would purchase me tobacco, and take my letters from the post-office for me; and, under these stipulations, I went to work again. I kept, in a great degree, sober for a few days; but felt, all the time, indescribably miserable, from the consciousness that all confidence in me had been lost, and that I was a suspected man. This impression nettled me to the quick, and, ere long, I began to feel indignant of the control exercised over me. I thought that as I had battled with the world, single-handed, for twelve years, and had received nothing (with one or two exceptions) but unkindness and misery, I had a right to do as I chose, without being watched wherever I went. My proud spirit would not brook this system of espionage, so I speedily made up my mind to do as I pleased. If I wanted drink, I considered I had a perfect right to gratify my inclinations, and drink I determined to have.

Have it I did, though secretly, and to my employers it was a matter of wonder how I managed to get drunk so

often. My funds, as I said, were all expended, and I was driven by my ravenous appetite to a course which, at any other time and under any other circumstances, I should have shrunk in horror from. I had in my possession some books which I once had valued, some of them presents; and I also retained a few articles, the once highly valued mementos of dear and departed friends. As I looked eagerly over these frail remnants of what I once possessed, my all-absorbing passion for drink exercised its tyrannizing power, and one by one, until none remained, every relic was disposed of, and the proceeds arising from the sale of them spent for rum. Could there be a more striking instance of the debasing influence which alcohol exerts? Why, at one time, I would almost as soon have parted with my life as with those precious remembrancers of

'The loved, the lost, the distant, and the dead.'

Now, however, all fine feeling was nearly obliterated from the tablet of my affections, and if I felt any pang in parting with articles I once so prized, the glass was my universal panacea. At length nothing remained on which I could raise a single cent, and I found in the lowest depths of poverty 'a lower still.'

I have, in several parts of this narrative, referred to my vocal talents and my ventriloquial acquirements. After every other resource had failed me, in my utmost need, I was compelled, as the only means of getting a little rum, to avail myself of these aids. Accordingly, my custom was to repair to the lowest grogshops, and there I might usually be found, night after night, telling facetious stories, singing comic songs, or turning books upside down and reading them whilst they were moving round, to the great delight and wonder of a set of loafers who supplied me with drink in return. Who would have recognized in the gibing mountebank, the circle of a laughing, drunken crowd, the son of religious parents, one who *had* been devoted and affectionate not so very long before; one, too, who had felt and appreciated the pleasures which religion alone can bestow? At times my former condition would flash across my mind, when, in the midst of riot and revelry, conviction would fasten its quivering arrow in my heart, making it bleed again, although I was forced to hide the wound. And through the mists of memory, my mother's face would often appear, just as it was when I stood by her knee and listened to lessons of wisdom and goodness, from her loving lips. I would see her mild reproving face, and seem to hear her warning voice; and, surrounded by my riotous companions, at certain seasons, reason would struggle for the throne whence she had been driven, and I would, whilst enjoying the loud plaudits of sots,

'See a hand they could not see,
Which beckoned me away.'

Sabbaths which, from my childhood, I had been taught to reverence, were now disregarded. Seldom did I enter God's house, where prayer was wont to be made, as I had done during a portion of the time I resided in New York. The day of rest was no Sabbath to me, and my usual way of spending it was to stroll into the country, where I might be alone, with a bottle of intoxicating liquid in my possession. When this was empty, I would crawl back to the town, under cover of the darkness, and close the sacred hours in some obscure groggery, in the society of those who, like myself, disregarded the command of the Almighty to keep holy the Sabbath day.

Again the dreary winter was about to resume its rigorous reign, and with horror I anticipated its approach. My stock of clothing was failing fast. I had no flannels or woollen socks, no extra coats, and no means of procuring those absolutely necessary preservatives against the severities of an American winter. I had no hope of ever becoming a respectable man again, — not the slightest, — for it appeared to me that every chance of restoration to decent society, and of reformation, was gone forever. I wished, and fully expected, soon to die. Hope had abandoned me here, and beyond the grave nothing appeared calculated to cheer my desponding spirit. O, what a deep and stinging sense I had of my own degraded position, for my feelings were keenly alive to the ridicule and contempt which never ceased to be heaped on me. Utterly wretched and abandoned, I have stood by the railway track with a vague wish to lie across it, drink myself into oblivion, and let the cars go over me. Once I stood by the rails, with a bottle of laudanum clattering against my lips, and had nearly been a suicide; but the mercy of God interposed, and I dashed the poison on the ground, and escaped the sin of self-murder. All night long have I lain on the damp grass which covered my wife's grave, steeped to the very lips in poverty, degradation, and misery; and yet I was a young man, whose energies, had they been rightly directed, might have enabled me to surmount difficulty, and command respect.

I had long since ceased to correspond with my sister, and so careless had I become, that I never thought of communicating again with the only relative I had remaining. Frequently was I tempted to take my life, and yet I clung instinctively to existence. Sleep was often a stranger to my eyelids, and many a night would I spend in the open air, sometimes in a miserable state of inebriation, and, at other times, in a half-sober condition. All this time I often resolved that I would drink no more —

that I would break the chain which bound me, but I still continued in the same course, breaking every promise made to myself and others, and continuing an object of scorn and contempt. I felt that very few, if any, pitied me, and that any should love me was entirely out of the question. Yet was I yearning intensely for sympathy; for, as I have before stated, my affections were naturally strong and deep; and often, as I lay in my solitary chamber, feeling how low I had sunk, and that no one eye ever dropped a tear of pity over my state, or would grow dim if I were laid in the grave, I have ardently wished that I might never see the morning light. Fancy, reader, what my agony must have been, when, with the assurance that no drunkard could enter the kingdom of Heaven, I was willing, nay, anxious, for the sake of escaping the tortures to which I was subjected in this life, to risk the awful realities of the unseen world. My punishment here was greater than I could bear. I had made a whip of scorpions, which perpetually lashed me. My name was a byeword. No man seemed to care for my soul. I was joined, like Israel of old, unto idols, and it seemed as if the Lord had said respecting me, 'Let him alone.'

Before I conclude this portion of my history, let me urge on every young man, whose eye may glance over these pages, to learn from my miserable state a lesson of wisdom. Let him beware of the liquor that intoxicates. Poets may sing of the Circean cup — praise in glowing terms the garlands which wreathe it — wit may lend its brilliant aid to celebrate it, and even learning invest it with a charm; but when the poet's song shall have died, and the garlands have all withered; when wit shall have ceased to sparkle, and the lore of ages be an unremembered thing; the baneful *effects* of the intoxicating draught will be felt;

and then will the words of wisdom be awfully verified in the miserable doom of the drunkard:—

'Wine is a mocker — strong drink is raging.'

*   *   *   *

'Who hath woe? who hath sorrow? who hath contentions? who hath wounds without cause? who hath redness of eyes?

'They that tarry long at the wine; they that go to seek mixed wine.

'Look not thou upon the wine when it is red, when it giveth its color in the cup, when it moveth itself aright.

'*At the last it biteth like a serpent, and stingeth like an adder.*'

AUTOBIOGRAPHY.

BY JOHN B. GOUGH.

PART SECOND.

Hitherto my career had been one of almost unmitigated woe; for, with the exception of the days of my childhood, my whole life had been one perpetual struggle against poverty and misery, in its worst forms. Thrown at a tender age upon the world, I was soon taught its hard lessons. Death had robbed me of my best earthly protector, and Providence cast my lot in a land thousands of miles from the place of my birth. Temptation had assailed me, and trusting to my own strength for support, I had fallen, O, how low! In the very depths of my desolation, wife and children had been torn from my side. In the midst of thousands I was lonely, and, abandoning hope, the only refuge which seemed open for me was the grave. A dark pall overhung that gloomy abode, which shut out every ray of hope; and although death to me would have been a 'leap in the dark,' I was willing to peril my immortal soul and blindly rush into the presence of my Maker. Like a stricken deer, I had no communion with my kind. Over every door of admission into the society of my fellow-men, the words, 'No Hope,' seemed to be inscribed. Despair was my companion, and perpetual degradation appeared to be my allotted doom. I was intensely wretched; and this dreadful state of things was of my own bringing about. I had no one but myself to blame for the sufferings which I endured; and when I thought of what I might have been, these inflictions were awful beyond conception. Lower in the scale of mental and moral degradation I could not well sink. Despised by all, I despised and hated in my turn, and doggedly flung back to the world the contempt and scorn which it so profusely heaped on my head.

Such was my pitiable state at this period — a state apparently beyond the hope of redemption. But a change was about to take place — a circumstance which eventually turned the whole current of my life into a new and unhoped for channel.

The month of October had nearly drawn to a close, and on its last Sunday evening I wandered out into the streets, pondering as well as I was able to do, for I was somewhat intoxicated, on my lone and friendless condition. My frame was much weakened by habitual indulgence in intoxicating liquor, and little fitted to bear the cold of winter, which had already begun to come on. But I had no means of protecting myself against the bitter blast, and as I anticipated my coming misery, I staggered along, houseless, aimless, and all but hopeless.

Some one tapped me on the shoulder. An unusual thing that, to occur to me; for no one now cared to come in contact with the wretched, shabby-looking drunkard. I was a disgrace — 'a living, walking disgrace.' I could scarcely believe my own senses when I turned and met a kind look; the thing was so unusual and so entirely unexpected, that I questioned the reality of it — but so it was.

It was the first touch of kindness which I had known for months; and simple, and trifling as the circumstance may appear to many, it went right to my heart, and like the wing of an angel troubled the waters in that stagnant pool of affection, and made them once more reflect a little of the light of human love.

The person who touched my shoulder was an entire stranger. I looked at him, wondering what his business was with me. Regarding me very earnestly, and apparently with much interest, he exclaimed:

'Mr. Gough, I believe?'

'That is my name,' I replied, and was passing on.

'You have been drinking to-day,' said the stranger, in a kind voice, which arrested my attention, and quite dispelled any anger at what I might otherwise have considered an officious interference in my affairs.

'Yes, sir,' I replied, 'I have.'

'Why do you not sign the pledge?' was the next query.

I considered for a minute or two, and then informed the strange friend, who had so unexpectedly interested himself in my behalf, that I had no hope of ever again becoming a sober man; that I was without a single friend in the world who cared for me, or what became of me — that I fully expected to die very soon — I cared not how soon — nor whether I died drunk or sober — and, in fact, that I was in a condition of utter recklessness.

The stranger regarded me with a benevolent look — took me by the arm, and asked me how I should like to be as I once was, respectable and esteemed, well clad, and sitting as I used to in a place of worship, enabled to meet my friends as in old times, and receive from them the pleasant nod of recognition as formerly — in fact, become a useful member of society?

'Oh!' replied I, 'I should like all these things first rate, but I have no expectation that such a thing will ever happen. Such a change cannot be possible.'

'Only sign our pledge,' remarked my friend, 'and I will warrant that it shall be so. Sign it, and I will introduce you myself to good friends, who will feel an interest in your welfare and take a pleasure in helping you to keep your good resolutions. Only, Mr. Gough, sign the pledge, and all will be as I have said; ay, and more too.'

Oh! how pleasantly fell these words of kindness and promise on my crushed and bruised heart. I had long been a stranger to feelings such as now awoke in my bosom. A chord had been touched which vibrated to the tone of love. Hope once more dawned, and I began to think, strange as it appeared, that such things as my friend promised me *might* come to pass. On the instant I resolved to try, at least, and said to the stranger:

'Well, I will sign it.'

'When?' he asked.

'I cannot do so to-night,' I replied, 'for I *must* have some more drink presently; but I certainly will to-morrow.'

'We have a temperance meeting to-morrow evening,' he said; 'Will you sign it then?'

'I will.'

'That is right,' said he, grasping my hand, 'I will be there to see you.'

'You shall,' I remarked; and we parted.

I went on my way much touched by the kind interest which, at last, some one had taken in my welfare. I said to myself, 'If it should be the last act of my life, I will perform my promise, and sign it even though I die in the attempt, for that man has placed confidence in me, and on that account I love him.' I then proceeded to a low groggery in Lincoln square hotel, and in the space of half an hour, drank four glasses of brandy; this, in addition to what I had taken before, made me very drunk, and I staggered home as well as I could. Arrived there, I threw myself on the bed and lay in a state of drunken insensibility until morning

The first thing which occurred to my mind on awaking was the promise I had made on the evening before, to sign the pledge; and feeling, as I usually did on the morning succeeding a drunken bout, wretched, and desolate, I was almost sorry that I had agreed to do so. My tongue was dry, my throat parched — my temples throbbed as if they would burst, and I had a horrible burning feeling in my stomach which almost maddened me and I felt that I *must* have some bitters or I should die. So I yielded to my appetite, which would not be appeased, and repaired to the same hotel, where I had squandered away so many shillings before; there I drank three or four times, until my nerves were a little strung, and then I went to work.

All that day, the coming event of the evening was continually before my mind's eye, and it seemed to me as if the appetite which had so long controlled me, exerted more power over me than ever. It grew stronger than I had at any time known it, now that I was about to rid myself of it. Until noon I struggled against its cravings, and then, unable to endure my misery any longer, I made some excuse for leaving the shop, and went nearly a mile from it in order to procure one more glass wherewith to appease the demon who so tortured me.

The day wore wearily away, and when evening came, I determined, in spite of many a hesitation, to perform the promise I had made to the stranger the night before. The meeting was to be held at the lower Town Hall, Worcester and thither, clad in an old brown surtout, closely buttoned up to my chin, that my ragged habiliments beneath might not be visible, I repaired. I took a place among the rest, and when an opportunity of speaking presented itself, I requested permission to be heard, which was readily granted.

When I stood up to relate my story, I was invited to the stand, to which I repaired; and, on turning to face the audience, I recognized my acquaintance who had asked me to sign. It was Mr. Joel Stratton. He greeted me with a smile of approbation, which nerved and strengthened me for my task, as I tremblingly observed every eye fixed upon me. I lifted my quivering hand, and then and there told what rum had done for me. I related how I was once respectable and happy, and had a home; but that now I was a houseless, miserable, scathed, diseased, and blighted outcast from society. I said, scarce a hope remained to me of ever becoming that which I once was; but having promised to sign the pledge, I had determined not to break my word, and would now affix my name to it. In my palsied hand I with difficulty grasped the pen, and, in characters almost as crooked as those of old Stephen Hopkins, I signed the total abstinence pledge, and resolved to free myself from the inexorable tyrant — rum.

Although still desponding and hopeless, I felt that I was relieved from a part of my heavy load. It was not because I deemed there was any supernatural power in the pledge, which would prevent my ever again falling into such depths of woe as I had already become acquainted with, but the feeling of relief arose from the honest desire I entertained to keep a good resolution. I had exerted a moral power, which had long remained lying by, perfectly useless. The very idea of what I had done, strengthened and encouraged me. Nor was this the only impulse given me to proceed in my new pathway: for many who witnessed my signing, and heard my simple statement, came forward kindly, grasped my hand, and expressed their satisfaction at the step I had taken. A new and better day seemed to have dawned upon me.

As I left the hall, agitated and enervated, I remember chuckling to myself, with great gratification, 'I have done it—I have done it.' There was a degree of pleasure in having put my foot on the head of the tyrant who had so long led me captive at his will; but, though I had 'scotched' the snake, I had not killed him, for every inch of his frame was full of venomous vitality, and I felt that all my caution was necessary to prevent his stinging me afresh.

I went home, retired to bed; but in vain did I try to sleep. I pondered upon the step I had taken, and passed a restless night. Knowing that I had voluntarily renounced drink, I endeavored to support my sufferings, and resist the incessant craving of my remorseless appetite as well as I could; but the struggle to overcome it was insupportably painful. When I got up in the morning, my brain seemed as though it would burst with the intensity of its agony, my throat appeared as if it were on fire, and in my stomach I experienced a dreadful burning sensation, as if the fires of the pit had been kindled there. My hands trembled so, that to raise water to my feverish lips was almost impossible. I craved, literally gasped, for my accustomed stimulus, and felt that I should die if I did not have it; but I persevered in my resolve, and withstood the temptations which assailed me on every hand.

Still, during all this frightful time, I experienced a feeling, somewhat akin to satisfaction, at the position I had taken. I had made at least one step towards reformation. I began to think that it was barely possible that I might see better days, and once more hold up my head in society. Such feelings as these would alternate with gloomy forebodings, and 'thick coming fancies' of approaching ill. At one time hope, and at another fear, would predominate; but the raging, dreadful, continued thirst was always present, to torture and tempt me.

After breakfast, I proceeded to the shop where I was employed, feeling dreadfully ill. I determined, however, to put a bold face on the matter, and, in spite of the cloud which seemed to hang over me, to attempt work. I was exceedingly weak, and fancied, as I almost reeled about the shop, that every eye was fixed upon me suspiciously, although I exerted myself to the utmost to conceal my agitation. How I got through that day, I cannot now tell, but its length seemed interminable, and as if it would never come to an end. I felt I was undeserving of confidence after I had so often broken my promises of amendment; but I determined to make another effort to procure the respect of my employers, and going to one of the gentlemen in the shop, I informed him that I had signed the pledge.

He looked at me very earnestly, and said, 'I know you have.'

'And,' I added, 'I mean to keep it.'

'So they all say,' he replied; 'and I hope you will.'

As he spoke doubtingly, I reiterated my determination to abide by the resolution I had made, never more to touch intoxicating liquors, and said to him, 'You have no confidence in me, sir.

'None, whatever,' he replied; 'but I hope you will keep your pledge.'

I turned to work again, saddened in mind and subdued in spirit; for the conversation I had just held with my employer showed me how low I had sunk in the esteem of prudent and sober-minded men. Whilst brooding over my misfortunes, I heard my name mentioned, and, turning round, saw a gentleman, who had entered unobserved by me. He said, 'Good morning, Mr. Gough. I was very glad to see you take the position you did last night, and so were many of our temperance friends. It is just such men as you that we want, and I have no doubt but you will be the means of doing the cause a great deal of good.'

This greatly encouraged me; and the gentleman, whose name was Mr. Jesse W. Goodrich, then and now practising as an attorney and counsellor at law in Worcester, added, in a very kindly tone, 'My office is at the Exchange, Mr. Gough, and I shall be very happy to see you, whenever you like to call in, — very happy.

It would be impossible to describe how this act, trifling as it appeared, cheered me. With the exception of Mr. Joel Stratton, who was a waiter at the temperance hotel, and who had asked me to sign the pledge, no one had accosted me for months in a manner which would lead me to think any one cared for me, or what might be my fate. Now, however, I was not altogether alone in the world; there *was* a probability of my being rescued from the slough of despond, where I had so long been floundering. I saw that the fountain of human kindness was not utterly sealed up; and again a green spot, an oasis, small, indeed, but cheering, appeared in the desert of life. I had something now to live for. A new desire for life seemed suddenly to spring up; the universal boundary of human sympathy included even my wretched self in its cheering circle. And all these sensations were generated by a few kind words.

What a lesson of love should not this teach us? How know we, but some trifling sacrifice, some little act of kindness, some, it may be, unconsidered word, may heal a bruised heart, or cheer a drooping spirit. Never shall I forget the exquisite delight which I felt when first asked to call and see Mr. Goodrich; and how did I love him from my very heart for the pleasure he afforded me in the knowledge that *some one* on the broad face of the earth cared for me,—for me, who had given myself up as a castaway; who, two days before, had been friendless in the widest signification of the word, and willing, nay, wishing, to die. Any man who has suddenly broken off a habit, such as mine was, may imagine what my sufferings were during the week which followed my abandoning the use of alcohol. Any attempt to describe my feelings would inevitably fall far short of the reality, and I shall mention only one or two circumstances in connection with this eventful period of my life.

On the evening of the day following that on which I signed the pledge, I went straight home from my workshop, with a dreadful feeling of some impending calamity haunting me. In spite of the encouragement I had received, the presentiment of coming evil was so strong, that it bowed me almost to the dust with apprehension. The unslakable thirst still clung to me, and water instead of allaying it, seemed only to increase its intensity. I feared another attack of delirium tremens, and not without reason; for, on that very evening, when I took the iron pin to screw up the binding-press, it seemed to turn to a writhing, creeping snake in my hands. I dropped it in horror, and it was nothing but a bar of iron! These and similar illusions terrified me, and ere long my worst apprehensions were realized. I was fated to encounter one struggle more with my enemy before I became free.

Fearful was that struggle. God, in his mercy, forbid that any other young man should endure but a tenth part of the torture which racked my frame and agonized my heart. As, in the former attack, horrible faces glared upon me from the walls,—faces ever changing, and displaying new and still more horrible features,—black, bloated insects crawled over my face, and myriads of burning, concentric rings were revolving incessantly. At one moment the chamber appeared as red as blood, and in a twinkling it was dark as the charnel-house. I seemed to have a knife with hundreds of blades in my hand, every blade driven through the flesh of my hands, and all were so inextricably bent and tangled together, that I could not withdraw them for some time; and when I did, from my lacerated fingers the bloody fibres would stretch out all quivering with life. After a frightful paroxysm of this kind, I would start like a maniac from my bed, and beg for life, life! What I of late thought so worthless, seemed now to be of unappreciable value. I dreaded to die, and clung to existence, as feeling that my soul's salvation depended on a little more of life. A great portion of this time I spent alone; no mother's hand was near to wipe the big drops of perspiration from my brow; no kind voice cheered me in my solitude. Alone I encountered all the host of demoniac forms which crowded my chamber. No one witnessed my agonies, or counted my woes, and yet I recovered; *how*, still remains a mystery to myself, and still more mysterious was the fact of my concealing my sufferings from every mortal eye.

In about a week, I gained, in a great degree, the mastery over my accursed appetite; but the strife had made me dreadfully weak. Gradually my health improved, my spirits recovered, and I ceased to despair. Once more was I enabled to crawl into the sunshine; but, O! how changed.

Wan cheeks and hollow eyes, feeble limbs, and almost powerless hands, plainly enough indicated that, between me and death, there had indeed been but a step.

A great change now took place in my condition for the better, and it appeared likely enough that the anticipations of my friend, Mr. Stratton, who induced me to sign the pledge, as to my becoming once more a respectable man, were about to be realized. For a long period, of late, I had ceased to take any care with respect to my personal appearance, for the intemperate man is seldom neat; but I now began to feel a little more pride on this head, and endeavored to make my scanty wardrobe appear to the best advantage. I also applied myself more diligently to business, and became enabled to purchase articles which I had long needed, and assume a more respectable appearance. Unfortunately, however, work soon began to slacken, and my circumstances, in consequence, were but poor.

I, generally, regularly attended the weekly temperance meetings, and my case being well known, I was at length invited to speak on the subject. After some hesitation, I consented to do so, and addressed an audience for about fifteen minutes, stating what my course had been, and what temperance had effected for me, and also expressing my firm determination to adhere to the total abstinence pledge. I well remember the individual who first engaged me for a regular speech. It was a good man, and devoted friend of the cause, Mr. Hiram Fowler, of Upton. He heard my address at one of the temperance meetings, and thinking I should do good, was very anxious to secure my humble services.

One afternoon, not long after I joined the society, a gentleman invited me to speak on temperance, in the schoolhouse, on Burncoat plain. That evening I shall never forget. I was not, from scarcity of funds, enabled to procure fittiny habiliments in which to appear before a respectable audience, and so I was compelled to wear an old overcoat, which the state of my under clothing obliged me to button closely up to my chin. The place assigned to me was very near a large and well-heated stove. As I spoke, I grew warm, and after using a little exertion, the heat became so insufferable, that I was drenched in perspiration. My situation was ludicrous in the extreme. I could not, in consequence of the crowd, retreat from the tremendous fire, and unbuttoning my coat was out of the question altogether. What with the warmth imparted by my subject, and that which proceeded from the stove, I was fairly between two fires. When I had done my speech, I was all but done myself, for my body contained a greater quantity of caloric than it had ever possessed before or since. I question whether Monsieur Chabert, the fire king, was ever subjected to a more 'fiery trial.'

Not long after this, it began to be whispered about that I had some talents for public speaking; and my career, as an intemperate man, having been notorious, a little curiosity as to my addresses was excited. I was invited to visit Milbury, and deliver an address there. I went, in company with Doctor Hunting, of Worcester. Mr. Van Wagner, better known, perhaps, as the Poughkeepsie blacksmith, was also to speak. I spoke, for the first time, from a pulpit at this place; and my address, which was listened to very attentively, occupied about a quarter of an hour or twenty minutes. At this time, nothing was farther from my intentions than becoming a public speaker. In my wildest flights, I never dreamed of this. I can sincerely say that I was urged to give these early addresses solely by a hope that good, through my instrumentality, might be done to the temperance cause, to which I owed my redemption.

Prior to delivering this address at Milbury, I had purchased a new suit of clothes, the first which I had been able to get for a long period. They came home on the day fixed for my speaking. Now, I had been so long accustomed to my old garments, that they had become, as it were, a part and parcel of myself, and seemed to belong to me, and feel as natural as my skin did. My new suit was very fashionably cut, and as I put on the articles, one by one, I felt more awkwardness than, I verily believe, I ever exhibited, before or since, in the course of my life. The pantaloons were strapped down, over feet which had long been used to freedom, and I feared to walk in my usual manner, lest they should *go* at the knee. I feared, too, lest a strap should give, and make me lop-sided for life. The vest certainly set off my waist to the best advantage; but it did not seem, on a first acquaintance, half so comfortable as my ancient friend, although the latter had long been threadbare, and *minus* a few buttons. And, then, the smartly cut coat was so neatly and closely fitted to the arms, and the shoulders, and the back, that, when it was on, I felt in a fix as well as a fit. I was fearful of any thing but a mincing motion, and my arms had a cataleptic appearance. Every step I took was a matter of anxiety, lest an unlucky rip should derange my smartness. How I tried the pockets, over and over again, and stared at myself in the glass! Verily I felt more awkward, for some time, in my new suit, than I did whilst roasting before the fire in my old one.

On the evening following my visit to Milbury, I delivered a second address, in another church there, which was well attended. Invitations now began to pour in on me from many quarters, and I had been asked, several times, to go to the same old school-house, on Burncoat plain, where I had before spoken; when, on the 26th of December, 1842, Dr. Kendall, of Stirling, applied for some person to deliver a temperance address. I was recommended as a suitable person, and went with him, occupying the whole of the evening, for the first time. Mr. Van Wagner spoke the next night, and I was detained until the Sunday morning. On my return to Worcester, I found that several applications for my services had been made from other towns. Mr. Genery Twichell was desirous that I should go with him to Barre, where a New Year's Day celebration, or temperance jubilee, consisting of singing and addresses, was to be held. In compliance with Mr. Twichell's wish, I attended the anniversary, and felt much gratification; after which I again returned to Worcester.

I now, finding that my engagements were increasing fast, applied to my employers for leave of absence for a week or two, in order to enable me to perform them. The required permission I obtained. When I went away, I left a pile of Bibles on my bench unfinished, promising to finish them on my return; but unforeseen circumstances occurred, and I never returned to complete them.

My time was now almost entirely employed in lecturing on the temperance cause; and, as good appeared to be effected by my labors, I was encouraged to proceed. I visited, about this time, in succession, the towns of Grafton, Webster, Leicester, Milbury, West Boylston, Berlin, Bolton, Upton, Hopkinton, and Mendon, together with many other places in Worcester county, the names of which it is not necessary to record. My audiences gradually increased in numbers, and, as I acquired more confidence in speaking, my labors were rendered the more useful and acceptable.

I must now refer to a circumstance which occurred about

five months after I signed the pledge, and which caused infinite pain to myself, and uneasiness to the friends of the cause. I allude to a fact, notorious at the time — my violation of the pledge. This narrative purports to be a veritable record of my history, and God forbid that I should conceal or misstate any material circumstance connected with it. If the former portion of this Autobiography be calculated to operate as a warning against the use of alcoholic liquors, the event which I am now about to record may not be without its use, in convincing many who have flung away the maddening draught, that they need a strength, not their own, to enable them to adhere to the vows they make. Well, and wisely, has it been said by the inspired penman, 'Let him that thinketh he standeth, take heed lest he fall;' for unassisted human strength is utterly unable to afford adequate support in the hour of weakness or temptation. We are only so far safe when we depend on a mightier arm than our own for support. Our very strength lies in our sense of weakness, and this was to be demonstrated in my experience.

I had known all the misery which intoxication produces, and, remembering it, could fervently offer up a prayer, such as the following, which, although first breathed by other lips than mine, aptly expressed my feelings : —

'ALMIGHTY GOD, if it be thy will that man should suffer, whatever seemeth good in thy sight impose on me. Let the bread of affliction be given me to eat. Take from me the friends of my confidence. Let the cold hut of poverty be my dwelling-place, and the wasting hand of disease inflict its painful torments. Let me sow in the whirlwind, and reap in the storm. Let those have me in derision who are younger than I. Let the passing away of my welfare be like the fleeting of a cloud, and the shouts of my enemies be like the rushing of waters. When I anticipate good, let evil annoy me; when I look for light, let darkness come upon me. Let the terrors of death be ever before me. Do all this, but save me, merciful God, save me from the fate of a Drunkard. Amen.'

I loved the temperance pledge. No one *could* value it more than I; for, standing, as I did, a redeemed man, enabled to hold up my head in society, I owed every thing to it. Painful as I said this event of my life was in the act, and humiliating in the contemplation, I proceed to state every particular respecting it.

I was, at this time, delivering addresses in the town of Charlton, Worcester county. Laboring so indefatigably, and indeed unceasingly, almost immediately, and for some time, after suddenly breaking off the use of a stimulus to which I had been accustomed for years, I became very weak in health; and, being of an extremely nervous temperament, I suffered much more than I otherwise should have done. I had an almost constant hæmorrhage from my stomach, and gradually became so excited, and nervously irritable, that I entirely lost my appetite, and could neither eat nor sleep. The engagements that I had made at Charlton came to a termination on Fast day, and in order to prepare for an address the next evening at Sutton, that town being the next on my list of appointments (numbering now more than thirty in succession), I returned to Worcester. Whilst there, and on my way there from Charlton, I felt sensations to which I had before been a stranger. It was a most distressing feeling, but one impossible to define. It will be remembered that, in a former page, I have given an account of an accident which I received when a boy, my head having been wounded by a spade. In the neighborhood of this old injury I experienced considerable pain. A restlessness, too, accompanied these symptoms, for which I could not account, and which I could not by any effort subdue. It was noticed, with some uneasiness, by my friends, that I acted and talked very strangely; but I was not at all conscious that, in my every day habits, there was any thing to excite or attract more than ordinary attention.

I boarded with a Mrs. Chamberlain, as good, kind, and considerate a woman as I ever knew. She observed my illness, and strongly urged me to remain at home, and go to bed. But I was in so nervous a state, that to remain still for five minutes together was a thing utterly impossible. I could neither sit in one position long, or remain standing; and this restless feeling was far more distressing to myself than can be imagined by those who have not suffered in a similar way. It appeared to me that I must be going *somewhere*, I knew not, and cared not whither, but there was a certain impulsive feeling which I could not restrain, any more than an automaton can remain motionless when its machinery is wound up. I left Mrs. Chamberlain's house, much against her wish, saying I should return shortly, and intending to do so; but when I had wandered about for a little time, I heard the fifteen-minute bell, at the depôt, announce that the train was about to start for Boston, and almost without thinking of what I was about to do, I proceeded to the station, entered the cars, and, without any earthly aim or object, set out for Boston; all I felt was an irresistible inclination to move on, I cared not where.

Several gentlemen, into whose company I fell, noticed the extreme strangeness of my deportment and conversation whilst in the cars. On arriving in Boston, I strolled for some time about the streets, uncertain how to employ or amuse myself. Evening drew on, and it occurred to me that I might dissipate my melancholy, and quiet myself down, by going to the theatre; I resolved to pursue this course, and accordingly entered the playhouse. I had not been there long before I fell in with some old companions, with whom I had been intimate many years before. We talked together of old times; and, at last, observing my manner, and noticing that I talked strangely and incoherently, they inquired what ailed me. I told them that I felt as if I wanted to move on, that move on I must, but cared not whither,—in fact that I was very ill. After being pressed to accompany them and take some oysters, I consented, and we all repaired to an oyster-room. It was during the time of taking this refreshment that a glass of wine or brandy was offered me. Without thought, I drank it off. And then, suddenly, the terrible thought flashed across my mind that I had violated my pledge. The horror I felt at the moment, it would be impossible for me to describe. Ruin, inevitable ruin, stared me in the face. By one rash and inconsiderate act, I had undone the work of months, betrayed the confidence reposed in me by friends, and blasted every hope for the future. To say that I felt miserable, would only give a faint idea of my state. For five months I had battled with my enemy, and defied him when he appeared armed with all his terrors; but now, when I fondly fancied him a conquered foe, and had sung in the broad face of day my pæans of victory, to hundreds and thousands of listeners, he had craftily wrought my downfall. I was like some bark,

> 'Which stood the storm when winds were rough,
> But in a sunny hour, fell off;
> Like ships that have gone down at sea
> When heaven was all tranquillity.'

My accursed appetite, too, which I deemed eradicated, I found had only slept; the single glass I had taken roused my powerful and now successful enemy. I argued with myself that as I *had* made one false step, matters could not be made worse by taking a few more. So, yielding to temptation, I swallowed three or four more potations, and slept that night at the hotel. With the morning reflection came; and fearful, indeed, appeared to me my situation. Without drinking again, I started in the cars for Newburyport, painfully feeling but not exhibiting any signs of having indulged in the intemperate cup on the previous evening. At Newburyport an unlooked for trial awaited me,—I was invited to speak for the temperance society there. I felt that I had no claim *now* to be heard, although I bitterly repented my retrograde movement; but at length I consented to speak, and did so, both on the Sunday and the following Monday. To Worcester I dreaded returning, so agonized was I in mind. It was there I came forward as a redeemed drunkard, had there, time and again, solemnly vowed that the intoxicating cup should never press my lips again, had there been received by the kind and the good with open arms, and encouraged to proceed; but, alas! how had I fallen! and with what countenance could I meet those to whose respect and sympathy I felt I had now no longer claim?

I returned, in consequence of entertaining such sentiments as these, again to Boston, there intending to remain until I should decide as to what my future course should be. I became faint, hungry, and sick; and my heart remained 'ill at ease.' Again I drank, although not to excess, and at length resolved, at all hazards, to return to Worcester, which place I reached on Saturday, where, as might be expected from my conduct previous to leaving, my friends were very much alarmed at my absence.

On my arrival home, I immediately sent for my friend, Mr. Jesse W. Goodrich, the same gentleman, it will be remembered, who kindly invited me to call on him the day after I signed the pledge. I also sent for Dr. Hunting, who had greatly interested himself in my welfare. When these gentlemen came to see me, I at once made them acquainted with what had transpired in Boston, and my violation of the pledge, and then expressed to them my determination to leave the town, county, and State, never more to return to it. I then re-signed the pledge, and commenced packing up my books and clothes, with the full determination of leaving Worcester the following Monday.

My friends, who did not desert me, even in these dark hours of my existence, again rallied round me, and persuaded me to remain, in order to attend the temperance meeting on the Monday I had fixed as the day of my departure. My candid statement had, in a measure, revived their confidence in me. In accordance with their desires, I did remain, and went, at the time mentioned, to the upper Town Hall, where a very large audience was assembled, who appeared to feel a great interest in the proceedings. I was almost broken-hearted, and felt as if I were insane; but I humbly trust that I sincerely repented of the false step I had taken, and, cheered by the considerate kindness of my friends, I determined, God helping me, to be more than ever an uncompromising foe to alcohol.

As this portion of my history is of some importance, I shall, instead of entering into any detailed description of the meeting I have just spoken of myself, quote in this place the report of the proceedings which appeared at the time in the public journals.

The following article appeared in the 'Cataract and Washingtonian:'—

'Mr. John B. Gough, as soon as he was known to be in the hall, was called for in all directions, and received in a manner which showed the true spirit of Washingtonian sympathy, kindness, and charity, to be still predominant in the bosom of this great Washingtonian fraternity. Feeble in health, and with an utterance half choked by the intensity of his feelings, he briefly alluded to, and promptly acknowledged his late misfortune, saying that he *had*, within a few days past, deemed himself a crushed and a ruined man; but that the enemies of the great cause he had attempted to advocate need not rejoice. That he had rallied, had re-signed the pledge, and then felt, and should prove himself, a more uncompromising foe to alcohol than he had ever been before; and, after invoking, in tones that came *from* and went *to* the heart, the blessing of Heaven upon his friends, this society, and the cause, attended by his physician and some friends, retired from the hall, subdued, even to tears, by the trying ordeal through which he had been passing.'

The following is extracted from a more extended report in the same journal:—

'The Washingtonian Society of Westboro' met at the Town Hall, on Thursday evening, April 20, 1843. The hall was full to overflowing. The meeting was called to order by the President of the Society, and opened with prayer by the Rev. Mr. Harvey; after which the President introduced Mr. J. B. Gough, the well-known, eloquent, and successful advocate of temperance, who, in a very feeling and appropriate manner, stated that, within a short time, he had broken his pledge, but he had signed it again, again risen up to combat King Alcohol, and that he appeared before them the uncompromising foe to alcohol in all its forms, willing to devote all the energies of his body and mind to the noble cause of temperance; and, with all humility, threw himself upon the kindness of his friends, stating it was for them to say whether or not he should proceed, and have their kindness and support, when the following resolutions were offered, and unanimously adopted, almost by acclamation:—

'" *Resolved*, That as intemperance is the cause of most of the misery and suffering that affect our fellow-men, drying up and poisoning the streams of domestic happiness, it is therefore our imperative duty to exert our united efforts against the monster, and stand, shoulder to shoulder, until the evil is banished from the land.

'" *Resolved*, That we highly appreciate the former services of Mr. J. B. Gough, as a Washingtonian lecturer, and, notwithstanding the unhappy circumstances which have lately occurred, we do most cordially greet him in the Washingtonian spirit of kindness and sympathy, and most cheerfully do we give him our countenance and support in the glorious cause of temperance."

'Mr. Gough again rose, evidently much embarrassed, and was received by the audience with *decided* marks of approbation. He stated, that to be thus received was more than he felt able to bear. Scorn and contumely he should be enabled to endure, but to kindness he had not always been accustomed, and he was completely unmanned. Recovering his self-possession, he went on, and most eloquently warned all, particularly the young men, who had become Washingtonians, *to abandon their old associates*, and not place themselves *in the way of temptation.* He portrayed, in most glowing colors, the criminality of those who endeavor, whatever may be their motive, to induce any one to violate his pledge, leaving them to their own consciences and their God. After holding the undivided attention of his audience for near an hour, he concluded with a most powerful appeal to all to come out and sign the pledge, hoping that no one would offer as an excuse, that the speaker had violated his, but come out, and, each and all, give their support to a cause which is worthy of the best effort of our powers.'

A similar resolution was passed at Sutton It was as follows: —

'*Resolved*, That we deeply sympathize with Mr. Gough in his misfortune, in having violated his pledge, and heartily express our satisfaction with his apology, and highly approve of his determination to continue his labors in the temperance cause.'

Never shall I forget the kindness shown me at this time by my friends, amongst whom I would especially mention Mr. Goodrich, Dr. Hunting, and Mr. George M. Rice, of Worcester.* It would be impossible for me to enumerate here all from whom I received the most considerate attentions, but they are not forgotten by me, and never will be.

Although freely and fully forgiven by the Society, I still felt keenly on the subject of my lapse; but my inten-

---

* Although by the generosity of my friends I was kindly forgiven, yet by some few I was, and still am, regarded in no very favorable light. I regret this, but do not blame them for not recognizing me on the true Washingtonian principles; they have my good will and wishes, whatever may be their disposition towards me.

tion of leaving the town was not carried into effect; as my friends, one and all, urging me to remain, I felt it my duty to accede to their wishes. I was waited upon in Worcester by Mr. Ellsworth Childs, of Westborough, with a request from the good friends of that place that I should visit them, and I felt it to be a duty to go to the different towns where I had made engagements, and to which I had been reinvited, freely and frankly to confess the circumstances which led me to break my appointments, and solicit their forgiveness, which was willingly accorded in every case.

I trust that I now had a full sense of my own insufficiency to keep myself from sinking. Hitherto I had relied too implicitly on my own strength for support, and my utter weakness had been painfully exemplified in my violation of a sacred promise. It was a humiliating blow, but it taught me that I derived my strength from on high, and that when He withdrew it I was utterly powerless to think of myself any good thing. Whatever my future situation in life may be, I hope ever to possess a strong sense of my utter weakness, and cherish a humble dependence on Him who is able to keep me from falling, and render my labors honorable and useful.

This account of my violation of the pledge will, I doubt not, be entirely new to many of my readers, although in my own neighborhood the fact was notorious enough. It is my earnest wish to send forth this narrative to the world in as complete and perfect a manner as practicable; omitting nothing, nor adding to any thing, so that it may be as faithful a record of my life as can be presented. I have not shrunk from depicting the dark days of my life, because I wished to warn my fellow-men against the wine-cup, and to strip the false and fading flowers from the manacles which amuse the inebriate whilst they cripple his energies; and in referring, as I shall have occasion to do, in the remaining pages, to the time since the dark pall was lifted up, I trust, forever, and hope's brilliant star shed on me its lustre, I hope I shall not be deemed egotistical — than this nothing can be more foreign to my views and sentiments. My readers must take the picture as it is, remembering that I have not adopted the style of any academy or school, but endeavored to present to the mind's eye a graphic delineation of what may be often met with in our daily paths — a painting of human nature FROM THE LIFE.

AUTOBIOGRAPHY.

BY JOHN B. GOUGH.

PART THIRD

WITH the exception of about three or four weeks of the summer of 1843, I have labored since that year in behalf of the temperance cause, having, I trust, sought and obtained assistance from on High, and rested all my hopes for success on the right foundation.

The sphere of my operations soon became extended, and I delivered lectures in the counties of Worcester, Norfolk, Middlesex, and sometimes in the border towns of Connecticut, Vermont, New Hampshire, and as far as Providence, Rhode Island. During this period I had received repeated invitations from a gentleman well known in Boston, Moses Grant, Esq., to go to that city and deliver addresses there. I felt, however, no disposition to accept his offer at this time; but sometime afterward, on the 23d of August, 1843, happening to be at a celebration at the village of Hopkinton, Massachusetts, Mr. Grant came to me and requested a sight of my book of appointments. I showed him what he required, and he immediately placed his finger on the sixteenth, twenty-first, twenty-second, and twenty-third days of September, and told me I must consider myself engaged by him for those days. Mr. Grant then very kindly told me to come to his house, and divest myself of all fear, for a good opportunity should be given me. I accordingly agreed with Mr. Grant to visit Boston, and on Saturday, the sixteenth of September, proceeded to that city, and went at once to Mr. Grant's house, where I was very kindly received.

I felt rather apprehensive in view of speaking in Boston, for I had heard it spoken of as the modern Athens, and knew that as to intelligence it stood very high amongst the cities of the Union. It was of no use, however, to look back; and as I was announced to speak that same evening at the Tremont Chapel, under the Museum, I determined to pluck up my courage. As I walked towards the Chapel I really felt half inclined to run away. On entering the house I found it about half full. I had frequently stood up before much larger audiences, but I never experienced so much hesitation and nervous sensibility as then. My courage, like that of Bob Acres, seemed to be oozing out at the palms of my hands, and my heart palpitated with apprehension. But I managed to get through the ordeal, for such in reality it was, without my trepidation having been much observed.

On the four next following days I spoke at Roxbury, and on the twenty-first I delivered an address again in Boston, at the Rev. Mr. Turnbull's church, in Harrison avenue. On each of the two next days I spoke in Marlboro' Chapel; although I had heard much of temperance meetings being frequently held there, I had never seen them. On the first night I spoke there it was about half full, and on the next the audience filled the building.

I then left Boston, and travelled through the various towns in the vicinity, delivering addresses, until the following third of November, when I returned to the city, and spoke three or four times at Marlboro' Chapel, and, on five or six occasions, at the Odeon. I felt some diffidence about speaking at the latter place, fearing it was too large for me, but, to my surprise, on Sunday night it was very full, and on the Monday evening crowded to excess. This reception encouraged me, and I continued to give addresses in Boston, with very few exceptions, until the second of December, when I went to Portland, Maine, and again returned to Boston, speaking in the course of the month, sometimes for the Washingtonians, and at others for the Ladies' Benevolent Society, but principally under the direction of my friend, Deacon Grant, and the Boston Temperance Society, then under the judicious management of that gentleman, who acted and still acts as its President. My services were now in requisition at Concord, N. H., New Bedford, Nashua, Gloucester, Marblehead, Rockport; and I made a trip into the Old Colony of Plymouth, where the Pilgrim Fathers landed, and visited also the towns of Newburyport, Newport, R. I., and many other places, returning occasionally to the city, and speaking to large audiences there.

I was married at Worcester, on the 24th of November, 1843, by the Rev. Mr. Smally, a gentleman who, from the first, had been my friend. After this, I went to reside at Roxbury, where we boarded with Mrs. Fuller, a warm-hearted Washingtonian, one ever ready to assist the reformed man; in consequence of which, her house somewhat resembled a hospital, or place of refuge for the destitute. Mrs. Fuller evinced her love to the cause, by often being out of pocket, through her endeavors to promote it.

Through Deacon Grant and other gentlemen, I received applications for my services from the cities of New York, Philadelphia, Richmond, Va., Charleston, S. C., Cincinnati,

Bangor, and many other distant places. After mature consideration, it was decided by my friends that I should first visit New York, accompanied by Deacon Grant, as the anniversary of the American Temperance Union was to be held in that city. We left Boston on the 8th of May, 1844, and I delivered an address in New York at the anniversary on the ninth; and on the tenth and twelfth of the same month I spoke in two of the churches. I also paid a visit to Newark and to the city of Brooklyn, and on the 16th of May started for Philadelphia, in which city, although arrangements had been made for my speaking, it was not deemed advisable to hold meetings, in consequence of the riots which had recently occurred there. I then proceeded to Baltimore, in which city I spoke for five nights; thence I went to Washington, where I delivered addresses in the morning and evening, and, returning, gave four lectures in Philadelphia, and two in New York. Whilst proceeding to Boston, in order to be present at the grand temperance celebration on the thirtieth of May, I delivered an address on board the steamer Massachusetts, in company with Dr. Patton, the Rev. John Marsh, and many other friends of the cause.

Before I allude to the magnificent demonstration, just referred to, I would mention, that I have received several testimonials of the approbation and good-will of kind friends. Let it be perfectly understood, that I do not make any mention of them from a feeling of pride, or in a spirit of self-satisfied egotism. It is rather in acknowledgment of the kindness of the respected donors that I take any notice of these mementos here. I extract the following from the Boston Bee:—

'The exercises at the Tremont Temple, on Thursday evening, on occasion of Mr. Gough's farewell address, [previous to leaving with Deacon Grant for Philadelphia,] were highly interesting, and attended by a large audience. The singing by the Euterpeans, Quartette Club, and others, was excellent, and Mr. Gough's address exceeded in interest all his former efforts. An elegant silver medal was presented to Mr. Gough, accompanied by some eloquent remarks by the Rev. E. H. Chapin, which called forth from Mr. Gough an off-hand expression of gratitude, sincere, warm, and gushing. We have been favored with an inspection of the medal which is certainly very beautiful. The workmanship is equal to any thing of the kind we ever saw, and was executed by Dennison, Adams & Co., 67 Washington street. On one side of the medal are the following words: —

PRESENTED
TO
JOHN B. GOUGH,
BY THE
BOSTON QUARTETTE CLUB,
AT THE
TREMONT TEMPLE,
MAY 2, 1844.

On the reverse is a fountain playing from a shell, beneath which is inscribed,

'THE FOUNTAIN OF LIFE.'

This is enclosed with very tastefully designed and executed scroll-work, and around the edge is engraved the names of the donors,

F. A. LYDSTON,   W. H. BURBECK,
S. P. CURRIER,   J. B. HECTOR.'

The edge of the medal is massive, and elegantly chased. Its value we presume to be somewhere between fifteen and twenty dollars intrinsically, but we cannot calculate its worth to the recipient, who has so well deserved such a compliment by his untiring and successful efforts in the cause of temperance.'

I returned to Boston early on the morning of the 30th of May, Mr. Samuel A. Walker having made arrangements for me to take a part in the exercises of the day, — a day which will long be remembered as one of the most interesting that ever occurred in the capital of Massachusetts. To my great surprise, I found on my arrival, that a barouche and four white horses had been prepared to convey me into the city. I experienced immense difficulty in getting to the State House, so dense was the crowd of persons in the various streets; and the whole population of the city, seemed almost to a man, to have risen up and hailed the celebration of the Genius of Temperance.

It was a brilliant day, in the most beautiful of the months; and all heaven and earth seemed to conspire in order to do honor to a cause whose object was the promotion of the happiness of God's creatures. The sun shone from a sky of cloudless azure, and the young May flowers rejoiced in his beams. The river sparkled as it flowed along, bearing on its broad bosom majestic barks, decorated, from trucks to main-chains, with gay flags and streamers. Every now and then, a light cloud of white smoke would float upward, and then the thunder of cannonading would reverberate amongst the distant hills. Music sent forth its glad tones upon the air, and as one band ceased its melody, another and another would burst forth, until the whole air was vocal with sweet sounds.

The city was dressed in gay attire, as we may suppose Venice was clad in her bright and palmy days. The shops were closed, for innocent pleasure ruled in the marts of commerce for a few short hours. The Custom House doors no more afforded egress and ingress to the busy sons of traffic; and at the banks was heard no silver sounds proceeding from the money-changers. The counting-house was still, for the merchant and his clerks had closed the ledger, and determined to balance accounts with temperance for once in the year, at least. From many a warehouse window, high up, hung gayly-colored fancy goods; and in some streets, lines of banners stretched across the streets from end to end, and hundreds of emblematic bottles were displayed, suspended, bottom upward, from lines, with the corks out.

From every window which commanded a view of the procession, gazed hundreds of old and young, grave and gay. Those in Washington street were crowded with ladies; and never did brighter eyes rest on a fairer scene than was presented to the view that day. It was a great day for the women.

Yes; for the women! They were more interested in such a demonstration than at first glance might be supposed. If ever an angel conveyed to *them* 'good tidings,' surely it must have been the heavenly visitant who bore temperance to their homes. Weak, delicate women may well bless a cause so pregnant with household blessings and domestic affections. How many bright eyes have grown dim, and light hearts heavy, and delicate frames bowed down to the dust — and what young hopes have been blighted, and strong affections crushed, and fair prospects blasted, during the absence of temperance from the hearthside. Ay, that hearth itself has become a desolate place, a domestic desert, barren and unprofitable; for, where the mother sang to her girl, and the father proudly gazed on his boy — where husband and wife 'took sweet counsel together,' and sister and mother formed the social ring, scarcely a link of the shivered chain is left to tell where happiness once had been. Families become scattered whenever intemperance plants his burning foot on the threshold, and that which was once —

'A little heaven below,'

a sanctuary from the toil and turmoil of this working day world, becomes but a cage of unclean birds — a very Pandemonium. Home! the magic of that word is dispelled forever, and they who dwelt under the family roof tree —

'Who grew in beauty, side by side,
Who filled one house with glee,
From each are severed far and wide,
By stream, and mount, and sea.'

O! has not woman reason to bless the temperance cause!

But to the procession; for, as no record of it, except the ephemeral reports of the newspapers, exists, I have been induced to notice it here.

I had witnessed many great gatherings, of various descriptions; but none ever affected me as this did. I could scarcely speak, and to describe my feelings would be impossible. Such a day I never, in my most sanguine dreams, imagined would have dawned on earth.

On it came, a dense, gayly-adorned, moving multitude, all in perfect order — every eye beaming with gladness, and every lip wreathed with smiles. The Boston Brigade Band came first, pealing forth strains of triumphant music. The Washington Light Infantry, clad in the trappings of war, next marched to celebrate the peaceful triumphs of temperance: and then a magnificent prize-banner displayed its gorgeous folds to the breeze. [This flag was afterwards awarded, by Moses Kimball, Esq., of the Museum, to the county having the largest number in the procession, according to its population.]

Then came a four-horse barouche, with two marshals, one on either side, in which was that truly great and good man, Governor Briggs, the President of the day, accompanied by the President of the Washingtonian Temperance Society. High as was his situation as Governor of the Bay State, never stood he in a prouder position than on that day. O! it was a noble thing, to see one who possessed such influence, exerting it in so noble a cause, and there, by his presence, encouraging the progress of a reform, the blessings resulting from which will only be known in that day when all secrets shall be revealed. A far nobler and more imposing sight was it than fields of martial glory could ever exhibit — fields where heroes stood, and received their laurels of triumph. The Governor of Massachusetts headed an army, which only pressed on to achieve bloodless victories, and proclaim 'peace on earth.' Such men constitute the true nobility. Universal benevolence is emblazoned on their escutcheons. The happiness of mankind, temporal and eternal, form their mottoes; and the gratitude and admiration of their kind, the rich seals to their patents of nobility.

In the carriage with the Governor were the Rev. John Marsh, W. K. Mitchell, and Wm. R. Stacy, Esq. The Vice-President of the day came next, and then followed a Reverend band of men, who, whilst they labored in their vocation for the interests of religion, acknowledged temperance as its handmaid. A large band of invited guests then formed its portion of the procession.

Next came the different societies of Suffolk county, with

banners streaming in the air, and music pealing from the Washingtonian Temperance Band, who honored the proceedings of the day by appearing for the first time in a new and splendid uniform. The band preceded the Parent Washingtonian Total Abstinence Society, which was incorporated with the North End Temperance Association, the West Boston Hancock Washingtonian Temperance Society, and the Fort Hill Washingtonian Temperance Society. After these came, in long and noble array, the Boston Temperance Society. Then, the South Boston Washington Total Abstinence Society. This body having conspicuously in their midst a Well of pure cold water, drawn by horses. The Chelsea Temperance Union next made its cheerful appearance; and then the St. Mary's Temperance Society, and the South End Washingtonian Benevolent Total Abstinence Society, preceded by the magnificent Band of the United States ship of the line Ohio. The Boston Marine Total Abstinence Society next followed, composed of hale, joyous-looking tars, who belied in appearance the assertion that grog was necessary for sailors. These bore in their ranks a splendid model of the United States Frigate Constitution, behind which came the crew of the United States ship Ohio.

That interesting body, the Boston Young Men's Total Abstinence Society, together with the West Boston Young Men's Total Abstinence Society, marched proudly on, followed by the Hibernian Total Abstinence Society. The Father Mathew Total Abstinence Society, the South Boston Catholic Total Abstinence Society, the South End Young Men's Benevolent Total Abstinence Society, the North End Youth's Total Abstinence Society; and then came a joyous band of children, forming the South End

Cold Water Army, and another legion of little ones — the Cold Water Army from Fort Hill.

A pleasant sight it was — that array of children, as with tiny feet they marched along the crowded streets, looking up to the vast multitude who gazed on them, with sparkling eyes, and delighted smiles. Some were there who had once known the misery of having a drunken parent; who had long been strangers to the kind word and approving smile, but who now felt all the blessed influences which temperance spread around. And happily the little things trooped on, waving mimic banners, and shouting for very joy. Some had fathers and brothers in that long line of procession, who never saw their little darlings so happy before. O! it was a happy sight.

This Cold Water Army had a leader, who ably

'Marshalled them the way that they should go.'

It was Deacon Grant, the friend of children. He had not, like many commanders of great armies, cannon at his beck, and bayonets to perform his bidding. He did not issue bulletins or general orders; but he was well supplied (as, by the way, he generally is, with tracts, and pamphlets, and handbills, in such vast and incredible numbers, all on the subject of temperance, that it is almost a mystery how he stows them away in his many pockets. Look at him, now that he is wound up to a pitch of enthusiasm, seldom equalled, and which it would seem never can be surpassed, waving, not a marshall's baton, but a beaver hat, the capacious interior of which, has, by an ingenious device, been converted into a teetotal library — a circulating one too, for see how the printed sheets are flying in all directions! Hurrah! shout the children in ecstasy — all of them are delighted and pleased with Deacon Grant's care of and for them; and as pleased and happy as any one of his little battalion is Deacon Grant himself.

The Fireman's Total Abstinence Association follow, as also other societies, according to the date of their formations. Glittering regalia announce the presence of the Independent Order of Rechabites, whilst loudly around them the Providence Brass Band echoes its exciting music. Following the band comes a delegation from Rhode Island; then, another band of music; then, a delegation from Maine, and embassies of peace from other States, which concludes the Suffolk county portion of the procession.

Middlesex sends forth its multitudes of total abstainers. Essex swells the triumphal throng, and the President and Vice-President of the County Temperance Society march in its midst. Worcester county is not behindhand — nor Hampshire — nor Hampden — nor Berkshire. Bristol county is up and doing, and, preceded by the New Bedford Brass Band, comes a Washingtonian whaleboat, on wheels, fully manned by stalwart looking fellows, who have taken up the harpoon of temperance with which to transfix the monster alcohol. Following Barnstable, Nantucket, and Dukes county, comes Norfolk, a small county, &c., then the Boston Brass Band finely playing. The Roxbury Artillery form an escort, and the different total abstinence societies and associations of the county bring up the rear.

It would be an idle thing to attempt a description or enumeration of the many devices which appeared on the banners and flags displayed in the procession, which consisted, at a moderate computation, of forty or fifty thousand persons. It was altogether a magnificent sight, and one which had never been paralleled. I saw one man in the long line who called up emotions of thankful interest in my heart. Some time before, that person came to me at my house in Roxbury, a wretched, drunken, broken-down creature, and signed the pledge. When he had done so, the poor fellow clasped his hands, and said, 'O! Mr. Gough, do you think I can keep it — do you think I shall be able to perform my promise?' I assured him that he could, and he expressed his earnest intention to adhere to his pledge. I now saw that very man, with a firm step and a flash of honest pride in his eye, bearing aloft a mottoed banner. He was a free man, and rejoiced in his emancipation. O! my heart thrilled with joy as I gazed, and knew and felt that hundreds such as he were joining in the festival of the day. Men who had been redeemed from a worse than Egyptian thraldom, and were restored to their homes, to their families, and to society. As banner after banner, with their various mottoes, passed by me, my feelings were strung to an almost painful degree of tension; for I remembered all the past, and could not help contrasting my present situation with what it had been.

The good city of Boston never witnessed a prouder array in her streets, than on that day. As the procession passed through the various streets, it was hailed with joyous acclamations; and, in many places, bouquets and garlands of flowers were showered from the windows by their fair occupants. When it arrived at the entrance to the spacious Common, the little great Cold Water Army filed off in two parallel lines, and between them went the long train of living beings to the place of appointment.

The old Common was all alive that day; from the dome of the State House floated the stars and stripes, the gorgeous folds of the national flag appearing in full relief against a sky of dazzling azure. Banners appeared in every direction, and the deep boom of the drum resounded from all quarters. During the intervals of music there was almost a Sabbath stillness, although from sixty to seventy thousand persons were present. The most perfect order was preserved, and nothing tended to mar the peaceful proceedings of the time. The mighty mass assembled around stands which had been erected on the Common, and a prayer having been offered up, in which blessings were implored on the great cause of temperance, the united voices of the vast assemblage, a noble band of freemen, arose to heaven, in a shout of, 'We're a band of freemen! We're a band of freemen!'

When the voices had ceased, Governor Briggs arose, and expressed in eloquent terms his high gratification at the spectacle before him; such an one, he hesitated not to say, as had never been witnessed in the world before. His Excellency spoke for more than half an hour, and his remarks elicited loud and frequent plaudits. The Governor was followed by other speakers, whose addresses were listened to with deep interest. It was a glorious thing to see men who stood in high places, and enjoying the confidence of the wise and good, taking conspicuous parts in such proceedings; and if angels ever rejoice over earthly scenes, surely it might have been whilst contemplating such a great moral spectacle.

As I was much fatigued by my labors during the past few weeks, I did not take any part in the proceedings of the day, at least in the open air. Indeed, I do not think I *could* have spoken at that time; my heart was too full. An engagement, however, had been made for me to speak in the Tremont Temple in the evening, to which place an admission fee of twenty-five cents was demanded, for the purpose of defraying expenses. The house was filled to overflowing, as soon as the doors were opened. The Governor, myself, and several others there delivered addresses, which closed the exercises of the day.

I cannot conclude this sketch of the proceedings of this memorable time, without paying a passing and well-deserved tribute to the chief-marshal, Samuel A. Walker, Esq., who so efficiently superintended the complicated arrangements of the procession, and by his liberal expenditure, conduced so much to its successful issue. From me, however, no commendation of one who has always been ready and willing to assist the cause of temperance, and who has frequently shown me personal kindness, is needed.

Having concluded arrangements with the Rev. John Marsh, of New York, secretary of the Am. Temp. Union, to travel with him to various towns and States of the Union, and deliver temperance addresses; after visiting Concord, Manchester, and Providence, we started, on the 24th of June, for western New York. I left Boston, for Hudson, on the 24th of June, and remained absent until the following third of August, having had a delightful tour, during which I enjoyed the high gratification of seeing the Falls of Niagara; which wonder of the world I will not venture to describe, for the very prudent reason that, as many have attempted to, and miserably failed, it would be of little use for me to add one to the list of incapables in this respect.

After my return to Boston, I spoke on Sunday, August 4th, at the Tremont Temple; and then, finding that my continued labors were somewhat exhausting my physical powers, which were not naturally of a powerful cast, I rested for six days, to recruit my energies.

I now paid visits to several of the surrounding towns, until the 11th of September, when I started again for Gardiner, Hallowell, Augusta, Bath, and Bangor. At the latter place, temperance prayer-meetings were held, at which ministers of all denominations attended, and appeared to feel great interest in the welfare of the glorious cause. A blessing seemed to follow these exercises; for, after I had delivered eleven addresses, seventeen hundred persons signed the total abstinence pledge. I shall never forget the many kindnesses I experienced from friends at Bangor. Whilst there, I remained at the house of Mr. F. Temple Wheeler, who, together with his excellent and amiable lady, secured to me every comfort; indeed, I do not remember having spent a week so pleasantly in every respect since I have been laboring in the temperance cause, as at this place. I believe much profit resulted to the mission and myself from the visit to Bangor. I must not forget to add, that Mr. William Dow, Mr. Duren, Mrs. Ingraham, and indeed a host of others, manifested a deep interest in my welfare and that of the great cause, of which I am a humble advocate.

At Bangor, I was presented with an elegant annual. The following report I extract from a Bangor paper:—

'MR. GOUGH AND THE LADIES.

'We have before stated, that the ladies made Mr. Gough, on Friday afternoon last, at the close of his address at the Hammond street church, two beautiful presents, as "mementoes of their affectionate regard." Mrs. F. T. Wheeler was selected to make the presentation address, which she did with a lady-like grace, peculiarly her own. The ladies most active in setting the matter on foot are entitled to much praise, and we do not believe their generous affection could have selected, had they ransacked the country through, a more worthy individual than Mr. Gough as the recipient of their favors. We should like to call the names of several of the ladies we wot of, who have taken a very great interest in the present temperance movement, some of whom, we know, have been the means of doing much good, had we permission to do so. They may rest assured there are those who will never think of their names but with gratitude and affection. If it be not presumptuous, we will say to them persevere, — persevere.

'The following is Mrs. Wheeler's excellent and touching address, with which we have been kindly favored. To which Mr. Gough replied in a most feeling manner; stating, what is an honor to the ladies of Bangor, that from their hands he had received the first testimonial of the kind:—

"Mr. Gough,— The ladies of Bangor, from a deep sense of gratitude for the great and unparalleled good which has been effected by your eloquent and energetic appeals, and desirous that you should possess some testimony of their high estimation of your worth, do, through me, their representative, request your acceptance of this *Annual*, and that you will retain it as a memento of their affectionate regard; and when you shall hereafter open it, and your eyes fall upon its pages, may it remind you how signally — how *wonderfully* — it has pleased God to bless your labors in Bangor; and may it elevate your thoughts and feelings to Him who has made you the honored instrument of saving so many from the miseries of intemperance, and inducing our beloved young men to dash the maddening cup from their lips, and return to the more quiet scenes of happiness and peace.

'" The ladies have not been unmindful of the great sacrifice of domestic happiness, consequent upon your devotion to the cause of temperance and humanity, nor of the amiable, the Christian companion, who must share the honors to which you so eminently entitle yourself; they therefore request you, on your return, to present her this *Basket*; that she may be reminded by the gift, bestowed mutually on you both, that, in your future absence from her, she must be contented to share her blessings with her country; happy in the assurance that your efforts will be crowned with the blessings of Heaven, and the approbation of the Society which surrounds you; while the poor and perishing, saved by your exertions, shall rise up and bless you, and be stars in your crown of rejoicing, for ever and ever."

'The Annual bears the following inscription:—

PRESENTED

TO

MR. J B. GOUGH, BY THE LADIES OF BANGOR,

AS A

MEMENTO OF THEIR GRATITUDE

For his faithful perseverance in the Cause of Temperance.

'The centre of the silver basket is engraved thus:—

MR. AND MRS. J. B. GOUGH.

FROM THE LADIES OF BANGOR.   September 28, 1844.

'A very beautiful gold pencil-case was also forwarded to Mr. Gough, on the 30th ult., by some young ladies of this city, who are not pledged to the cause of temperance. Many other tokens of respect were received by Mr. Gough from gentlemen of the city.'

Returning through Portland, I returned to the city of Boston, where I delivered several addresses; after which I again visited Taunton. Here a grand temperance gathering took place, at which, addresses were delivered by Mr. Stanton, Dr. Jewett, and myself. Of one circumstance, connected with this celebration, the Taunton 'Dew-Drop' gives the following account:—

'An elegant Bible, purchased by the Ladies' Total Abstinence Society of this town, was then, on their behalf, presented to Mr. Gough, by Samuel L. Crocker, Esq., accompanied with the following neat and pertinent address:—

'"MY KIND FRIEND,— The ladies have honored me with the office of presenting to you, my dear sir, this beautiful token of their regard.

'"I trust I need not say, that, personally, I most fully sympathize with them in the feeling that prompted the gift; and that no one, more highly than myself, appreciates and loves the precious treasure that constitutes the gift.

'"The ability, earnestness, and feeling with which you have advocated the great and good cause of temperance amongst us, has enlisted in your behalf universal admiration and esteem, and has induced, on the part of the ladies, this offering — an offering of comparatively trifling pecuniary cost, and yet, in itself, a treasure of priceless value.

'"To the truths contained in this book are we mainly indebted for all that makes our life here upon earth agreeable and happy — to these truths *alone*, for all we hope for in the world beyond the grave, which endureth forever, and whither we are all hastening.

'"The great work to which you have devoted yourself, is peculiarly a Christian enterprise, based upon the principles of this book. So far as our action is in accordance with these principles — so far as we seek and follow the direction of its Divine Author, so far will our cause be furthered by his continued help, and blessed by his most gracious favor. And, on the contrary, whenever we depart from those principles, or fail to give them due prominence, we may be sure that we shall endanger, if we do not utterly destroy, the fair fabric we have raised.

'"In all your doings, but especially in the glorious cause of temperance, I beg you will take this blessed book for your guide — make it your counsellor and friend, and you can never err; but it will lead you safely through all your trials, temptations, and difficulties, enable you triumphantly to overcome them all, and finally point out to you the way to happiness and heaven."

'Mr. Gough replied in his usually happy manner. He most heartily thanked the ladies for this expression of their regard for him as a humble advocate of temperance. He alluded to the lessons which his good mother had taught him from that blessed book. Many of those passages he had treasured up in his memory; he had never forgotten them. In his very worst days, some of them would be fresh in his mind. After finishing his remarks to Mr. Crocker, and thanking the ladies again, he placed the Bible on the table, and proceeded with his remarks to the audience.'

I also visited Marblehead, Providence, and Worcester; and, on the twenty-first of November, I started for New York city, and lectured occasionally in that city and its vicinity. Whilst in that quarter, I remained at the house of the Rev. John Marsh, at Brooklyn, about a fortnight; and I cannot but bear my willing testimony to the uniform kindness I have always received from this gentleman; who, I have already stated, ably fills the highly responsible office of secretary to the American Temperance Union. To Mr. Marsh I owe much, for the judicious manner in which he arranged meetings which I was to address. Whilst at Brooklyn, I became acquainted with Mr. Hurlbut and Mr. Ripley, two gentlemen, than whom none have the cause of temperance more entirely at heart. Myself and my wife visited at Mr. Hurlbut's during a fortnight of our stay in Brooklyn, and received many proofs of their Christian kindness. Would there were many more such devoted friends of temperance, then indeed would 'the work go bravely on.' Before I left these valued friends, arrangements were made by them for holding meetings on Long Island.

Before I proceed further with my narrative, I would mention that, in addition to the testimonials I have already alluded to, I received from the Cold Water Army of Gardiner, a present of a Bible, and from the Young Ladies' Temperance Society of Boston, a Silver Cup. The following extract from the 'Fountain' journal, refers to the gift of the children:—

'Acting upon the suggestion of some two or three thorough going temperance young ladies of this village, the Cold Water Army of Gardiner, which by the way numbers more than a thousand, determined to express their good feelings by presenting him with a splendid copy of the Bible. Accordingly a meeting was called, and the little ones came together in great numbers, bringing with them their little contributions, which altogether made quite a respectable sum. With a part of this, the committee of the Army, Misses M. Dennis and E. Holman, purchased the present designed for Mr. Gough, and a portfolio for Deacon Grant. Mr. Gough was invited to meet the Army at the Methodist chapel. Notwithstanding the storm, a large number of children and friends of the cause were present. After a prayer by the Rev. Mr. Smart, Mr. J. Winnett, principal of the Lyceum, in behalf of the enthusiastic donors, presented Mr. Gough with the (if rightly esteemed) invaluable donation, accompanied with the following very appropriate address: —

"Br. GOUGH, — In behalf of the children of the Cold Water Army of Gardiner, I present you this Bible, as a small token of that sincere esteem and gratitude which they so fondly cherish towards you, for your faithful and untiring exertions in their behalf, during your recent visit among them.

"Please, Sir, to accept it; and while turning over and reading its sacred pages, remember that the most holy feelings have prompted the gift, and that it will be with the deepest joy that they will learn of your success in raising the inebriate from his sufferings and degradation, and throwing around the rising generation that mantle of peace and security, which should guard, shield, and protect them against all the evils that follow in the train of intemperance.

"And, further, remember, when your eyes shall rest upon this precious book, how many hearts are rejoicing in consequence of your faithful exertions in the cause of benevolence and humanity; and may the thought inspire you to persevere to the end. And, when God, in his providence, shall call you from this scene of your labors and the world, that you may rest in those blissful regions where there are joys unspeakable and full of glory, is the heartfelt wish of this little army."

Mr. Gough replied in a most interesting speech of three quarters of an hour's length. He thanked the children for this manifestation of their good-will, spoke of his own redemption from the pit into which a depraved appetite had cast him, contrasted the state of the drunkard with the prospective condition of the members of the different cold water armies in the country; related briefly to them his movements and success since he was in Gardiner before; spoke of the pleasure he anticipated in being the bearer of the present to Deacon Grant; again tendered his thanks; invoked the blessing of heaven upon the Cold Water Army, and then bade them a kind farewell.'

The 'Boston Mail' thus notices the presentation of the Cup:—

'On Thursday evening, the ceremony of presenting to Mr. Gough a Silver Cup, was performed at the Tremont Temple. This honor was conferred upon him by the Young Ladies' Temperance Society of Boston; and he received it with becoming grace, and made a very effective speech on the occasion.'

A Bible was also presented me, by three ladies of Philadelphia; and two volumes of 'Notes,' by the Reverend Albert Barnes, of Philadelphia — the author. I might mention many other marks of kindness which have been shown me; but, feeling that enough has been said on this subject, I forbear, again assuring the reader that nothing but a sense of grateful feeling towards the donors induced me to record them in this form.

At the request of a lady, named Sanderson, I was induced to visit that dreary abode of misery and crime — the Penitentiary on Blackwell's Island, near New York. Mrs. Sanderson, like the celebrated Mrs. Fry, of England, and Miss Dix, of America, devotes much of her time to, what would appear to some, the almost hopeless task of reforming the wretched beings who are consigned to this fearful place. In the language of the Superintendent of the Prison, 'she does more good than fifty men.' My object in going was to hold a temperance meeting. Soon after my arrival, the doors of the different cells, which are built in tiers, one over another, were opened, and the convicts, male and female (some eight hundred in number), were led into the large chapel of the Penitentiary, and informed by the keeper of the object of the meeting. His Honor, the Mayor, James Harper, Esq., occupied the pulpit, and one or two clergymen, and some other gentlemen, were present. The Boston Quartette Club attended, and performed several appropriate pieces of music.

It was a striking sight, that assemblage of men and women, of all ages and descriptions. There was the hardened criminal, and the youth who had only just commenced the career of crime — women who retained little of womanhood in their swollen and bloated features, and young girls, on whose countenances traces of beauty yet lingered, sat side by side : *all* had committed offences against the laws, and were enduring its punishment. Such an audience I never before stood up to address; the spectacle was fearfully interesting.

In noticing the service, the New York 'Sun' said:—

'At the early part of the meeting, the prisoners seemed rather indifferent to what was going on; but the first sound of Mr. Gough's voice had scarcely died away, ere their hardened countenances began to relax, and, in a few moments, every eye was riveted on the speaker, with an expression of the deepest interest. As he proceeded with his touching appeals, many a rough cheek was moistened with tears, and the words '*that's the truth*' were often nodded about the room, as plainly as if they had been spoken. The women, particularly, seemed much affected; and manifested less anxiety to conceal their feelings than the men. It may not be improper to mention, too, that the optics of our worthy chief magistrate were, at intervals, unusually red; but this might have been owing to the rough wind he had encountered in crossing the river, or to an improper adjustment of the spectacles on his benevolent nose.'

At the close of my address, His Honor requested those of the prisoners, who would like to have another temperance meeting held there some Sunday, to manifest it by raising their hands. Every hand in the room, apparently was instantly shown, and one poor fellow ventured to bawl out, 'Let's have one *every* Sunday.' I am informed, that, after I left the Penitentiary, several of the prisoners applied to the Superintendent, and requested permission to sign the pledge.

Principally through the suggestion and exertions of my kind and valued friends, Mr. Hurlbut and Mr. Ripley, of Brooklyn, a benefit was got up for me, on Christmas evening, at the Tabernacle, in Broadway, New York. The New York press took the matter in hand, and, almost without exception, did all in their power to promote the object in view. The attendance at the Tabernacle was very large, and fully answered its intended object. At its close, a series of resolutions were passed, which expressed approval of my efforts in the temperance cause, and a desire that I should again visit the city.

I again left New York for Boston; and, on the 29th of December, delivered another address, at the Tremont Temple, in that city, after which I proceeded to Taunton, where a meeting was held, at which I spoke, for the benefit of Mr.

Williams, editor of the Taunton 'Dew Drop,' a deserving little sheet, devoted to the interests of the temperance cause.

The year was now drawing to a close, and it was arranged that a grand meeting, in Faneuil Hall, should be held on its last evening. I was present, and delivered an address on the interesting occasion. The old 'Cradle of Liberty' contained a vast assemblage, and hundreds who were present felt that, since the dying year commenced, they had thrown off fetters which had long galled them, and were now blessed with freedom, in its noblest sense. Minds which had long bowed down in blind idolatry to the monster — rum, had been emancipated from its tyrannic rule, and now saw the old year, as it passed away, bearing with it the record of their liberty. Many were there, too, who had welcomed in that year with song and wine — who had wreathed about its young temples the garland which dissipation loves to twine, and sent it, as it were, reeling on its pathway towards the future; but who now watched it, departing forever, laden with ardent hopes, high resolves, and, better than either, fulfilled purposes. During that year, what changes had taken place. When the keen blasts of January howled round yonder dwelling, in the outskirts of this populous city, a pale, wan woman might have been sitting

'Plying her needle and thread,'

and as she pondered on the new year, just entered upon its existence, she looked forward to its months with no hope, and reverted to the past with no pleasure. The past! what had it written on the page of memory, to cheer her? He to whom her young vows were given — who had promised to love and cherish her, had all but deserted her — and had buried feeling and affection in the intoxicating cup.

One by one, every slender thread of comfort had snapped, and with them some fine heartstrings cracked too. Earth to her appeared but a long dreary desert, over which a miserable caravan was passing, from which each after the other, the wretched pilgrims turned away and died, far from the refreshing fountains for which they pined. And the partner of that lone woman was away bidding farewell to the old year, and welcoming the new with the poisonous cup, and the thoughtless toast, forgetting that every moment which floated by bore its record with it. That midnight scene might have been in the eye of the writer, who, in portraying such a scene of sorrow, says:—

> ' Within a chamber pale and dim,
>   A pale wan woman waits in vain,
> Through the long anxious hours for him,
>   Away:— In want, and wasting pain
> A babe upon her knee is pining,
> Its winning smiles all scared away;
> She almost hopes the sun's next ray
> May on its calm cold corse be shining.
> Poor watcher! He comes not; she dreams
> Perchance of her old home; and now
> Upstarting with a livid brow,
> Clasps the babe closer to her breast;
> That dying child, yet loved the best.'

But, lo! a marvellous change has been effected. One evening when she was thus wasting and watching, her husband came home, in a miserable state of intoxication. She bore all his ill-humor, ay, even his brutality; and she tended him, and cared for him, as only a woman can. Morning came, and still the half-stupefied drunkard lay on his bed; but that day, salvation, in a temporal, if not in a higher and better sense, came to his house. The white-robed angel—temperance—went there an unbidden guest; kind words were spoken—encouragement was afforded—the *pledge* was signed—the fetters were broken. O! what a change! Smiles once more beamed on the wife's brow, and the home became a home indeed.

Look at that man there in the crowd, who is shouting with all his might, after the speaker has uttered some remark which makes the old 'Cradle' ring again with applause; his eye is bright—his complexion is clear—his step is firm, and his hand is steady. A cheerful-looking woman is leaning on his arm, and well-dressed, cleanly children are by them (the youngest is in its father's arms, crowing and bawling with the best of them). Can that be the man who heralded in the year with intemperate glee? and that the woman who sat desolate indeed in her wretched garret? and those the children who were ragged, and miserable? Yes! and temperance wrought the change. O! there were many such trophies of its peaceful conquests in Faneuil Hall that night!

And I had my recollections, too, as I stood on that platform. What had I been, two or three years before? Why a houseless, homeless, inebriate! Penniless, friendless, and almost hopeless. Little recked I how the days, months, and years rolled on; I seized the winged moments as they passed and plunged them into the maddening bowl. A comic song was my Christmas carol. The old year was despatched with a Bacchanalian glee, and the new one hailed with uproarious mirth. I scarcely took 'note of time,' even from its loss; but by the grace of God a change had been effected, and there I stood, on the last evening of eighteen hundred and forty-four, a humble monument of his mercy, feeling, as I trust I ever shall feel, that out of my utter weakness He had in me perfected strength to stand up and be privileged to warn others of the dangers of indulging in that which intoxicates. Unto His name would I ascribe all the glory.

With the new year I continued my exertions in the temperance cause; but before I proceed further with this narrative, which now draws near to a conclusion, I perhaps may be allowed to mention the result of my labors up to this time. I do not refer to the matter for the purpose of seeking praise from man, which so far as it is unaccompanied by the blessing which cometh from on high, is to me utterly valueless, but merely as statistical facts which to many friends of the cause may not be without interest.

I find, from notes which I have kept ever since I commenced the work of temperance reform, that, from the 15th of May, 1843, to the 1st of January, 1845, I travelled more than twelve thousand miles, by land and water; delivered six hundred and five public addresses, in churches, halls, public buildings, and in the open air, one hundred and ten of which were in the city of Boston alone; and obtained thirty-one thousand seven hundred and sixty signatures to the total abstinence pledge.

In the commencement of the present year, I again visited New York, and from thence proceeded to Philadelphia. It will be remembered, that I was prevented from delivering addresses in the 'City of Brotherly Love,' on my first visit to it, by the occurrence of the disastrous riots there, but quiet had now been long restored.

I delivered my first address, on Sunday evening, the 5th of January, at the Rev. Mr. Ides, First Baptist church, to a large audience: several placed their names to the pledge. On the Monday, I spoke at the Rev. Mr. Stockton's church, but felt great difficulty in doing so, having taken a severe cold on my journey. My next address was given at the Rev. Albert Barnes's church, Washington square, the largest in Philadelphia: it was crowded. Dr. Ely's church, in Buttonwood street, was open for me next evening: here again was a crowded congregation. My cold had now become so troublesome, that I announced I should not speak on the morrow; but, when the next evening arrived, several gentlemen so earnestly desired me to attend at Dr. Wiley's church, that I complied with their request, and, although suffering much from cold, spoke for about an hour. On the following Sunday evening, I addressed the medical students who were in Philadelphia attending lectures at the various medical schools, at the Rev. Mr. Lord's church. In the afternoon of the day, I spoke to a large concourse of Sabbath-school children, in Mr. Barnes's church, which, as well as Mr. Lord's church in the evening, was crowded to excess.

On Monday evening, the 13th, there was an immense meeting in the saloon of the Chinese Museum. Some idea of the enthusiasm, which the cause excited, may be formed from a knowledge of the fact, that two thousand three hundred tickets of admission, at twenty-five cents each, were sold, and that hundreds were unable to obtain admission. I spoke at this meeting, and much good seemed to be effected. The next day, I addressed a very large audience at the Rev. Mr. Mason's, Methodist church. On Wednesday afternoon, as many aged persons and invalids, who could not get out in the evening, had expressed a desire to hear me, I gave an address, in Dr. McDowell's church, which was so crowded, that another meeting was organized in the basement, which was addressed by that venerable champion of temperance, Mr. Hunt. That afternoon, two hundred and sixty persons signed the pledge. In the evening, I spoke for the Boston Quartette Club, at the Assembly Rooms.

On Thursday evening, the 16th, the upper saloon of the Chinese Museum was filled to overflowing, at twenty-five cents per ticket, half of the proceeds being given to the poor. In addition to an address from myself, the Rev. Mr. Hunt spoke, and there was music and singing by Johnson's Band and the Boston Quartette Club.

I cannot cease speaking of this visit to Philadelphia, without expressing the high gratification I derived from it, both with regard to the impulse given to the temperance cause, and the personal kindness which I received from many friends there, amongst whom I feel great pleasure in mentioning the Rev. Albert Barnes, the erudite author of the 'Notes' on various portions of the Holy Scriptures. I received, also, from many other ministers of Philadelphia, great encouragement and Christian kindness, which I shall not easily forget.

After leaving Philadelphia, I visited and spoke at Newark, in Dr. Eddy's church, and then proceeded to New York. On this occasion, myself and wife visited G. C. Ripley, Esq., at Brooklyn, and enjoyed some delightful intercourse with him and his family, as well as with our kind friend, Mr. Hurlbut, at whose house I remained during a former visit.

At New York, I spoke, on Sunday, the 19th, in the Rev. Mr. Smith's church, Rivington street; on Monday, at the Rev. Mr. Mason's, in Broome street. On Tuesday, I accompanied Mr. Hurlbut and Mr. Ripley to Jamaica, where I spoke, and enjoyed a pleasant season. On the morning of the 22d, I accompanied the Rev. Mr. Marsh to the State Convention at Trenton, and spoke before the Legislature in the evening. The next day, I went to New Brunswick, and, after speaking at Dr. Richard's church, obtained eighty-five names to the pledge, and returned to Brooklyn next day.

I next visited Patterson, and spoke there on Sunday evening: two hundred names were affixed to the pledge. On my return to New York, I spoke at Dr. Skinner's church, more especially to the ladies, many of whom signed the pledge. On the evening of Tuesday, the 28th, I delivered an address for the benefit of the Orphan Asylum, Brooklyn; and the same evening spoke for a short time at the Broadway Tabernacle.

I afterwards delivered two farewell addresses, one at the New York Tabernacle, and the other at Brooklyn, and left for Boston on the last day of January. On Sunday evening, February 2d, I spoke at the Odeon; at the upper Town Hall, Worcester, on Monday, 3d; at the State House, before the Legislature, on Wednesday, the 5th; and at Faneuil Hall, on the 6th. On the 7th, I visited Concord, and gave an address at the opening of the Shepherd's Temperance House there. On the evening of Sunday, the 9th instant, I spoke, to a very full audience, at the Tremont Temple, and bade a farewell for some months. The next week was devoted to the rest which I absolutely required; and having, on Monday, the 17th, addressed the ladies of Boston, at Mr. Barrett's, in Chambers street, in the afternoon, I left my home, once more, on the following day; and, when then these pages meet the eye of the reader, I shall be in the South, humbly endeavoring to forward the good work.

Before I again return, if the Almighty Disposer of events shall spare my health and strength to me, I shall have visited Richmond, Washington, and other places and have fulfilled an engagement of four weeks on Long

Island, made for me by my friends, Messrs. Hurlbut and Ripley, than whom more devoted friends of the great temperance reform do not exist.

Before I bid the reader farewell, and it is high time that I should do so, having been so long 'harping on one string,' I have a few remarks to make, which I trust will be received in the spirit in which they are offered.

And, first, I would advert to a statement which has been made by certain parties, that I am no Washingtonian. Now, for what object such assertions have been industriously put forth, I am at a loss to determine, but that such is the case I have been assured. In reply to the charge, if charge it be, I answer that ever since I have been the public advocate of the temperance cause, I have enforced, as strongly as I possibly could, the necessity and policy of observing the law of kindness towards the unfortunate persons who have become the victims of intemperance. I have advocated moral suasion *alone*, and in its fullest extent, too, in the case of the drunkard. But with respect to the rumseller, who sells that which causes his fellow-man to become an inebriate — who, for the sake of acquiring wealth, places that within a man's reach that disqualifies him for exercising the reason with which his Maker endowed him, and reduces him to a grade far below the level of the beasts that perish — who *sells* him that which unfits him for discharging the duties of a man and a citizen, towards his family and his country, — I say with respect to such a man, who, when the startling truths of the case are pressed home to his heart and conscience, still persists in poisoning the streams of society at their very fountain heads, that different and more stringent measures should be adopted. In my opinion, and I say it in all love to the rumseller himself, he should be prevented by the strong arm of the law from endangering, from merely mercenary motives, the peace, the prosperity, and the morals of the community at large. I will labor heart and hand with my fellow-men in the attempt to rid our land of the monster intemperance. Let those who advocate moral suasion alone go only a part of the way with me in the crusade against it if they will. If they refuse to advance further, be it so; but I hold it to be my duty, my imperative duty, to proceed yet another step, even if I go alone, and throw another wall of protection around the wretched and almost helpless child of intemperance, by placing moral and legal restraint upon the hands, which, for the sake of dollars and cents, would administer to the cravings of his depraved appetite. As surely as effect follows cause, so certainly would drunkenness diminish and disappear altogether, if there were no drunkard makers. My motto is, 'reform it altogether.' Annihilate the traffic, and then, temptation removed, the poor inebriate would have no enemy left to vanquish, and be free indeed. If this be, as I believe it to be, a fair exposition of the Washingtonian creed, then am I a Washingtonian. I highly respect and esteem many who differ from me in my sentiments, and willingly would I work with such devoted men as John F. Coles, of Boston, Edgar K. Whittaker, Esq., of Needham, Samuel A. Walker, of Brookline, Capt. Samuel F. Holbrook, Dr. Channing, of Boston, and many others whom I could mention; but still my own conviction remains that moral suasion alone for the rumseller would be as useless in the effort to remove drunkenness, as it would be ridiculous to attempt to empty the ocean drop by drop.

In my narrative I have frequently adverted to the kindness of friends; some, in my days of adversity, showed me favors which I never shall forget, whilst this heart continues to beat. It has been my happiness and privilege to be enabled to cancel every obligation which I contracted, so far as pecuniary matters are concerned; but the debt of gratitude which I incurred in more than one instance, never can be repaid. To each and all who befriended me when there existed no earthly prospect of their kindness being requited, I shall ever feel indebted.

I feel it necessary here to mention, with regard to the head of the family, Mr. ————, with whom I left England, to state, that I believe him to have been kindly disposed towards me, and towards him I feel a Christian regard. This avowal is drawn from me because it has been reported that I have endeavored to produce a different impression.

Nor can I ever feel sufficiently thankful for the friends whom the Lord has provided me with. They need no acknowledgement or praise from me, but I cannot close this little volume without gratefully assuring them that they will ever have honored places in my heart of hearts. Amongst them, I may mention Deacon Grant, of Boston, who, through good and through ill report has ever been my firm and faithful friend. The Rev. John Marsh, of New York, to whom I owe many acknowledgments for his frequent direction and advice. The Rev. John Pierpont, the Rev. William B. Tappan, Mr. Mellen, Mr. Thompson, of Boston; Mr. J. L. F. Warren, of Brighton; Messrs. Williams, of Roxbury; Samuel D.

Davenport, Esq., and family, of Hopkinton, and many others whose names, if chronicled here would swell my little work far beyond it prescribed limits. To the Press of Boston, and of the country generally, I am under large and lasting obligations, for the kind and indulgent manner in which my name has been so often mentioned; and I cannot suffer this opportunity of thanking the members of it to pass by unheeded.

And now, in reviewing all the ways in which the Lord hath led me, I feel, and would express, how much I owe to Him, by whose grace 'I am what I am.' Left alone, and unprotected in a stranger land, he watched my footsteps, and inclined my heart, in some degree, to seek his face and favor; but mysterious are the dealings of his providence. I was left to myself. Temptation assailed me and I fell — O! how low. Misery was my constant companion for many months; but deeply as I had sunk in the estimation of the world, one still watched my footsteps and preserved me from ruin when trembling on the very verge of destruction. Then was his hand outstretched to save me, and life again seemed enlightened by God's approving smile. But I depended for support upon an arm of flesh — on a broken reed; and the Almighty, in his infinite wisdom, saw fit to humble me unto the very dust He showed me that without strength from on high, I was unequal to the conflict; and in the school of affliction, I trust he taught me how feeble were my resolves, and how fruitless my endeavors, whilst I built my hopes upon aught below the skies.

In my violation of the solemn pledge, I feel a humble consciousness that he who doeth all things well, saw fit to abase me, in order that every reliance on self might be scattered to the winds, and my feet placed upon the Rock of Ages, so that my goings might be established. I had failed to acknowledge him in all my ways, and his hand mercifully interposed to check the growth of those seeds of pride and worldly wisdom which had begun to germinate, and already threatened to choke the good seed which his grace had implanted. I trust that I recognized in this trial the dealings of a merciful Father's hand; and it is my fervent hope that, with whatever success he may be pleased to crown my labors, his may be all the glory. I would disclaim all power in and of myself, and desire earnestly the influences of his Holy Spirit, without which I feel I can do nothing.

A few words, and I have done. This little book may by chance fall into the hands of young persons, and Sabbath-school children. O! may it serve as a warning to young men! If they would be honorable, useful, and happy, I conjure them, by all that is holy, virtuous, and even what we call respectable, to 'tarry not at the wine.' God forbid that they should learn experience in the bitter school in which I was a scholar, and from which I was plucked as a brand from the burning. I have not written these pages for the mere purpose of gratifying curiosity; a higher motive has, I trust, influenced me; and O, how happy should I be, in hearing, at some future period, that only one young man had been arrested in his fatal career. My hope is that this book will be useful. And, if the blessing of God should follow a perusal of it, in but one case, I shall have reason for thankfulness that I penned it, through all eternity.

Let Sabbath-school children remember, that I, like them, once listened to the kind instructions of a teacher [whom, sixteen years after, I accidentally met in Brooklyn, at a friend's house.] Had I then had an opportunity of signing the temperance pledge, the misery of a drunkard's feelings would, most probably, have been spared me. Let every child *feel* that, by signing that pledge, he cannot, if he sacredly adheres to it, ever become intoxicated. I pray God that no Sabbath scholar, who reads my experience, will ever feel in their own persons, or experience what it has been mine to endure.

The concluding portion of this work, I have been compelled to leave in the hands of a friend, who has kindly engaged to prepare it for the press, during my unavoidable absence, for some months, from home. As he will speak for himself, with respect to the matter of it, I shall now lay down my pen, humbly relying for aid in my future endeavors to stem the tide of intemperance, on him, without whom all human effort is vain, and in whose strength we may fearlessly go forth to wage an exterminating war against all that is opposed to the coming of his glorious kingdom.

LIFE OF JOHN B. GOUGH.

PART THIRD.

THE readers of Mr. Gough's autobiography, and the still larger class to whom he has been made known by his public addresses, having expressed a desire for further facts with reference to Mr. Gough's life and labours than what have already appeared before the world, the following narrative has been drawn up, not to gratify an idle curiosity, but to stimulate, to interest, and instruct. Mr. Gough is public property—his history is the history of a cause—all that concerns him concerns it—his triumphs are its triumphs—the greater is his success, the greater is the success of a work as noble as any that ever fired a human heart, or required the entire devotion of a human life. It is by human agency that intemperance is to be grappled with and humanity saved. The history, then, of the Temperance Reform, as of that of all other reforms, is the history of individuals; and surely one of the most illustrious of these is the orator who left our shores a boy—who with his winged words became a name and power amidst the teeming millions of the new world, and who comes back to us a loved and honoured man to preach against the curse so extensive and fatal in our midst, and to teach the slave of habit how he can burst his fetters and become free.

Our aim is not to give a chronicle " dry as the remainder biscuit after a voyage" of what Mr. Gough has done, and where he has been. We do not even profess to give the facts as they occur in chronological order, and from our scanty knowledge we must necessarily omit much that is valuable, and that would repay our gathering up and attempting to record. We make no ambitious attempt to decide on Mr. Gough's merits, to assign him his proper place amidst orators living or dead, or even fully to detail a career which has been wonderful in the extreme, and would have been accounted such even in the days of romance; we aim in a sketchy and popular manner to supplement the autobiography, as it were, by adding to it such facts as we have seen and heard in connexion with Mr. Gough's subsequent career. This publication will not supplant that, it merely completes it, by bringing it down to the present time. Our little outline will thus supply a public want, and, we trust, do the public good: less we cannot be satisfied with—more we shall not attempt to achieve. In these days of universal reading, all we modestly request is a spare half-hour; at any rate, this we have a right to expect from the friends of the Temperance cause at least. So much, then, by way of preface—at once we begin.

One of the most singular incidents in Mr. Gough's career was the remarkable manner in which he discovered the existence of his father, respecting whom he had given up all expectation of ever hearing in this world. His finding him was as a resurrection from the grave. Never on this earth did the son expect to stand side by side with his father whom he long thought dead. While at Philadelphia, Mr. Gough received a letter from a gentleman, stating he was an Englishman — and that when a child he possessed all the advantages which a religious education could confer. He had been well brought up —well started in life; but all had been in vain, for his drinking habits had reduced him to the deepest poverty. He had been alienated from his family and friends—he was an outcast without human pity or aid —would Mr. Gough consent to an interview with him. We need not add the interview took place, and happily the outcast was induced to sign the pledge. Mr. Gough took him to New York, and thence to Boston, where he obtained lucrative employment, and by his talents and character and position, made his way into the best circles of the town. He lived with Mr. Gough, and when the latter moved from Boston to Roxbury, he still made Mr. G.'s house his home. In the autumn of the year he decided upon returning to England. Mr. Gough at that time was confined to his bed with sickness; he came to Mr. Gough's bed-side and said, all that he had he owed to him—his heart and purse were Mr. Gough's. His debt of gratitude was greater than could ever be repaid — could he do anything for Mr. Gough in England? The latter told him that he was not aware that he had any relatives living in England; he had a father, but he had not heard of him for seven years, and he supposed he must be dead; if so, Mr. Gough would like to learn the particulars of his decease and where his remains were interred: the last he had heard from his father was in 1837, notwithstanding Mr. Gough had repeatedly written. Mr. Gough gave his friend all necessary directions and he left. Three months afterwards he received a letter, from Sandgate, stating his friend had visited his native village—had seen the house in which Mr. Gough was born, and conversed with those who knew him as a boy, and hoped that at last he had a clue to his father. In the meanwhile Mr. Gough paid a visit to Virginia, and laboured in the chief towns, such as Richmond, Norfolk, Petersburg, and Lynchburg. He then lectured at Liberty, in Bedford county. At this latter place, Mr. Gough was seized with a dangerous attack of brain fever—his exertions overpowered his slender frame—his life hung as it were by a straw. For a time the fears of his friends were greater than their hopes; it seemed as if he were about to be lost for ever to the world. Fortunately Dr. Moseley, to whose house Mr. Gough had been removed, nursed and tended him as a brother. He sat up with him every other night himself; and so happily, though Mr. Gough's life was despaired of, and the news went abroad that he was dead, and even letters of condolence on her supposed loss were received by his wife; still, owing to the skilful care of his doctor, and the tender nursing of his wife, and the kind providence of God, Mr. Gough was brought back from the jaws of death to life and health and strength again. During his illness letters had arrived for him, and one of them was from the gentleman alluded to, stating that he was successfully prosecuting his enquiries, and that he trusted soon to send him some welcome intelligence.

Almost in the identical language of the Hebrew Joseph,

as he asked of his brethren, as they stood trembling before him, suppliants for bread, Mr. Gough asked, "Is your father well—the old man of whom ye spake, is he yet alive?" In telling this tale at a crowded meeting in Boston, the repetition of these few words from the Bible is described as having produced a most wonderful effect. Immediately upon Mr. Gough's recovery he proceeded to Boston and there found a letter from his father waiting is him, stating that the old man was in Chelsea Hospital in good health, and longing to see his son once more. He had been married again, but his wife had died, leaving him one child a boy five years old. Mr. Gough immediately entered into correspondence with his father, and as the latter still expressed a desire to see his son and his daughter, who was married and settled in Providence, Rhode Island, Mr. Gough supplied him with the necessary means for his removal to America, which took place in 1848, when, accompanied by his boy, he landed in the western world, and father and son once more met after a separation of twenty eventful years—years at any rate fruitful to one in rich experiences, out of which had grown wisdom and strength; pity for the tempted and fallen, and a desire to win them back to God and man, as he had, after years of sorrow and despair, been won. The father resided with the son; and when the latter came over to this country in 1853, he followed him in about three weeks, and at the present time is still residing in London, where the evening of his days has been cheered and sustained by the son who was so fearfully lost, and so miraculously found. In this world of ours the tide of life often leaves father and son apart, and they never meet—or meet as wrecks, shattered and undone. At one time it seemed as it would have been so in this case; happily it was ordered otherwise by Him, in whose hand our life and breath are, and whose are all our ways. Such are some of the interesting particulars relative to Mr. Gough's search of a father. It may be as well to add here, that the gentleman through whose inquiries the discovery was made, was the same gentleman who assisted Mr. Gough in the publication of his life—a work which has had so immense a sale both here and in America, and which has done so much, by awakening an interest as to the temperance orator, for the temperance cause itself.

Mr. Gough is another remarkable illustration of how difficult it is to judge by appearances. You would never imagine that he found any great difficulty in addressing audiences, so ready is his fancy, and so swift his flow of words. At times, however, it is not so. One would scarcely think it, and yet occasionally it is the fact, that Mr. Gough's nervousness is very great. On the platform it seems as if nothing could affect him,—as if he was equal to every emergency,—as if he was as much at home there as another man by his own fireside. The very reverse is the case. His nervousness and depression previous to addressing public audiences is sometimes of the most intense and distressing character. On one occasion, at Boston, where he had previously spoken 160 times, it so far overcame him as to create the utmost alarm in himself and friends. The oration was to be delivered on a Sunday evening, at Tremont Temple. All that day it weighed heavily on Mr. Gough's mind. It kept him from the sanctuary: he felt that he could not worship that day—that it would be a mockery for him to attempt to do so. As the time for commencing the meeting drew on, he and Mrs. Gough went to the appointed place. Mr. Gough reached the door,—his heart failed him, and he went away. A second time he made the attempt, and again turned back. At length he mustered up his courage, and amidst doubt and trembling and fear again reached the door. But it was with difficulty he did so, the crowd was so great. Every part of the vast building in which the meeting was held was occupied. "You can't come in; the place has been full this hour," said one of the officials. "I wish you could keep me out," was Mr. Gough's reply, as he managed to insinuate his slender body into the little space that was left. Having achieved this no easy matter, he found Deacon Grant, the president, waiting in a state of the utmost anxiety; for the orator was staying at his house, and he knew but too well the state of his mind. "I can say nothing to-night," said Mr. Gough. But it was too late to postpone the meeting. It was felt necessary that Mr. Gough should say something, and so, nevertheless, the proceedings began. The Rev. Mr. Cushman commenced with prayer; then came the music. Mr. Gough hoped that would help him, as it had often done, to thoughts and feelings worthy of the time and place; but now for once, for a wonder, that failed, and with trembling limbs and a sinking heart Mr. Gough rose to address the assembled mass. "Ladies and Gentlemen," he began, "I have nothing to say. It is not my fault I am before you to-night. I almost wish I could feel as a gentleman in New York told the people that he felt—that they were all so many cabbages. I wish I could feel so." Then, as if recollecting himself, Mr. Gough continued, "No, I do not!"— When he looked into their faces—when he saw them to be rational and immortal beings, and remembered how drink had debased and dragged down the loftiest and noblest minds, he could not feel so—he thanked God he could not feel so; and then, with a felicity of illustration, and a torrent of words of fire almost unequalled, Mr. Gough proceeded to show the influence of alcoholic drinks on all that is noble and sublime in man, and to warn his hearers against the fearful fascinations of the intoxicating cup. And as Mr. Gough went on, gathering strength, mounting higher every minute, till the height of his high argument was attained, and all hearers were melted by his irresistible power, the effect was electrical. Not a trace of nervousness or depression of spirits remained, and he sat down, after speaking for an hour and a-half almost as one inspired. Deacon Grant, who believed Mr. Gough was utterly unable to address the meeting, was loudest in his expressions of praise, and when it was all over said to Mr. Gough, "If ever you frighten me so again I will never forgive you." Perhaps we may add, that Mr. Gough would not be what he is if he had not these dark times. The man who can never be depressed is not the man who can ever rise. The mountain stream, at times so overwhelming, at times may be blocked up and turned from its course almost by a single straw.

One winter, while Mr. Gough was lecturing in New York, he perceived amongst his audience two gentlemen with faces that at once won from him his admiration and regard. After his address had terminated they were introduced to him. One of them was Mr. Gregory, of Cincinnati, a right noble advocate of every good cause. Nothing would satisfy him but Mr. Gough's visiting Cincinnati. He was then going back there, and he was determined to carry off Mr. Gough bodily with him. Mr. Gough hinted at other and prior engagements. Mr. Gregory made very light of them. At length, as Mr. Gough had received numerous invitations from Cincinnati, he resolved to follow Mr. Gregory. This was in the winter of 1849. The weather was not well adapted for travelling. Much of the country was new and strange to them, and Mr. and Mrs. Gough felt at times that they had gone on a wild-goose chase. Proceeding from Cumberland, in Maryland, they went in the midst of sleet and snow to Brownsville, on the Monongahela river, where they left the stage, the drivers of which had been remarkably profane, and the passengers in which had been equally so; and after a dreary ride of 80 miles across the mountains took the steamer to Pittsburg. It was a dangerous journey, for the ice was making fast in the river, and the winter was rapidly setting in. At Pittsburg Mr. Gough met with an incident which he often tells us, illustrative of the good effect of not travelling on the Sabbath. He got to Pittsburg on the Thursday. The next day a boat was about to start for Cincinnati: it was a favourable opportunity, as in Pittsburg he had no personal friends At the same time Mr. Gough felt, that, if he availed himself of it, it would compel him to break through his invariable practice of strictly observing the Sabbath as a day of sacred rest, and accordingly he declined going by it. It was fortunate he did, for the boat remained from the Friday till Monday blocked up by the ice within fifty miles of Pittsburg, and the passengers were almost frozen and starved with the cold and hunger. As Mr. Gough was thus detained at Pittsburg, some of the friends of the cause, hearing of his arrival, requested him to deliver an address on Friday evening, which he consented to do. Notwithstanding the notice was so short a very good audience was collected, and good effect produced. Nothing would satisfy the people but Mr. Gough's staying with them a week. They telegraphed to Cincinnati, and from Cincinnati the people telegraphed a message back, to the effect that Mr. Gough might stay at Pittsburg, and accordingly Mr. Gough set as usual to work. One meeting was so crowded that there was a cry that the large church in which it was held was giving way. A fearful panic took place, but happily no harm was done. Six thousand signed the pledge. This was encouraging, and the people of Pittsburg determined to keep Mr. Gough with them another week. Accordingly, they again telegraphed to Cincinnati, and the good people of Cincinnati again sent a favourable message back. Meetings were held every night; never had there been such excitement before. The intemperate were reclaimed. Those who would have become so were saved ere they had learnt the habit which of itself is so fearful a bondage.

Mr. Gough left Pittsburg with the best wishes and prayers of thousands of friends, and arrived in Cincinnati two weeks later than was anticipated. Mr. Gough's visit there was a memorable one. Altogether twenty-seven public meetings were held. One of them was a temperance prayer-meeting, at which an episcopal clergyman presided. One meeting was for children, at which ten thousand were present, and almost all of them total abstainers. Another was for young men. Mr. Gough addressed them with great excitement and effect; at the close he invited the young men who would sign the pledge to occupy the pulpit for that purpose. It was a platform pulpit; and up those pulpit stairs walked three hundred young men to resolve never more to taste the drunkard's drink. Five hundred of the audience besides took the pledge;—the first who did so was a spirit dealer. Then they held, besides, a meeting for firemen. In the United States the firemen are a class by themselves. They are supposed to be a very difficult class to get at. They are supposed to consist of all the rough and free and untameable spirits of the town. This arises partly from their organization, and partly from their calling being such as would suit the lovers of excitement and danger and adventure. The Fire Association is a voluntary one in many towns in the States. They are free from being called out as soldiers or jurymen, and agree to act as firemen for seven years, during which time they are bound to attend every fire that takes place by night or day. The corporation supplies them with a house and engines, and they are left free to themselves. They are controlled in no other way: they elect their own officers, and fines are imposed on them if, when a fire takes place, they do not hasten to put it out. Besides the firemen, there is a supplementary association, also voluntary, consisting of persons who are not regular firemen. Horses are not used in America, as with us; so that we may reckon the firemen are an important class. Well, this class Mr. Gough was invited to address. He went to them with but little expectation of doing them much good. All kinds of discouragement had been thrown in his way. Every one said it would be impossible ever to have a meeting. It turned out as every one said—that the meeting was attempted to be disturbed; and it turned out as no one said—that the meeting was successful, nevertheless. People cried "Fire, fire!" but not a fireman would move till the orator had done,—for they had made arrangements accordingly; and the result was, the firemen were most enthusiastic in the cause; they threw into it their heart and soul; they held temperance meetings in their engine houses; and to this day do they cherish the memory of Mr. Gough's visit amongst them. Soon after the elections came on, and the result showed that Mr. Gough's labours had not been in vain. In spite of 1500 coffee-house keepers — (these men sell spirits) — a majority of 3,000 decided against granting licenses.— (In America this matter is settled by the townspeople themselves, and not by the magistrates, as with us.)

Mr. Gough then went to Aurora, Indianapolis, and Indiana. He then made a tour through Ohio, part of New York, and so home again. But it is difficult to follow Mr. Gough's wanderings. It is more easy to say where he has not been than where he has. Almost all the great republic of the West he has visited, and taught to be familiar with his voice and theme. Ohio Mr. Gough has visited twice. In Virginia he twice made a tour of some months. When there he was introduced to new features of life, and found even in the slave something to which he could appeal, and something which could respond to his appeal. Mr. Gough found the heart of the negro was much the same as that of the white man; —that it was to be touched by truth, won by love, melted by fervent zeal. It was a new thing to Mr. Gough to have to address such audiences, but he found great pleasure in it, nevertheless. The negroes listened to him as a messenger from heaven, and hung upon his every word as if it was divine. All the feeling of their emotional natures was aroused from its very depths as the orator went on. In Norfolk, Petersburg, Charlotsville, and in other of the principal towns of Virginia, Mr. Gough gathered round him the slaves, to speak to them of a slavery more terrible than even theirs;—nor did he speak in vain. More influential—more cultivated audiences he might possibly have had;—more discriminating audiences never. Every word told; every allusion was understood; every appeal produced a practical effect. Amongst them, at any rate, it could not be said that Mr. Gough laboured in vain, nor spent his strength for nought. But sometimes he met with scenes of an almost ludicrous character, especially when the manifestations of negro feeling took place. At Richmond, for instance, where the slaves had a large temperance society, they held a public meeting, at which three thousand negroes of all shades of colour were present. The singing was admirable—nothing could be better, especially the manner in which their impromptu pieces were performed. But during the meeting, and while Mr. Gough was lecturing, they would burst out into exclamations such as would have been likely to upset the gravity, and to destroy the self-possession, of a less practised hand; and even to Mr. Gough himself the interruptions must have been strange and startling at first. "Dat's me!" "Amen!" "Yes, yes!" and similar exclamations on the part of an audience, are not supposed to be a very material assistance to the speaker. In one part of his speech Mr. Gough referred to a better land;—the allusion was caught up in an instant, and as the contagion extended, from line to line they chanted out, as with one voice—

"Amen! amen! my soul replies;
I'm bound to meet you in the skies,
　　And claim my mansion there.
Now here's my heart, and here's my hand,
To meet you in that happy land,
　　Where we shall part no more."

The effect was of the most singular kind, but it was the mode the negroes adopted of showing how the speaker had touched them, and it was appreciated accordingly. At the conclusion of the meeting one after another came up to Mr. Gough to shake his hands; as he did so, an old negro said, "Massa, me very much obliged to you for coming and speaking to we coloured people. I signed the pledge myself eight years ago, and it helps my 'ligion, and I found out dis—dat a man can't make calculations that will come right for time and for eternity, if he drink much liquor."

In consequence of numerous invitations Mr. Gough received, he went to Canada in 1850. He commenced his visit at Montreal, and while delivering a course of lectures there, Sir J. Alexander called and asked if Mr. Gough would address the military men in garrison. Mr. Gough was but too happy to do this, and, accordingly, met a portion of the 20th regiment, with their officers, in Gosport-street church. In consequence Mr. Gough was requested to pay a visit to the barracks, which he did: where he got 200 men to sign the pledge and received an address from the men through the commanding officer, Lieutenant-Colonel Horn. When in England, Mr. Gough met with some of the men belonging to the same regiment, who told him more than half had kept the pledge. When Mr. Gough left Montreal for Quebec, Lieut.-Colonel Hays waited on him, asking him to address the military there—a Highland regiment being at Cape Diamond, and the 19th regiment in garrison. We need not add Mr. Gough complied with the request, and in the Assembly Hall in which the address took place, there was a muster of nearly 600 men, and it was a fine sight to see them—these brave brawny sons of Mars—as the speaker held them spell-bound by his magic powers. Mr. Gough also addressed the military in Kingston and Toronto, to which places he made a second and a third visit—proceeded down the Ottawa across to Prescott and Brockville, on to Hamilton and London, and then returned to New York by Niagara. In 1851 Mr. Gough visited Halifax and Nova Scotia, at which latter place he had an opportunity of addressing the famous 42nd Highlanders, many of whom are now out in the Crimea, and are still abstainers; and, if we may believe all we hear, all the better for it. While addressing the Highlanders, Mr. Gough told them he had seen a disgraceful sight that day; in his walks about the town he had seen the picture of a drunken Highlander drinking toddy, as the sign for an inn. He asked them if that was not too bad—if it was not a shame to put such a reflection on them over the door. He asked them if any publican dared put up the sign of a drunken lawyer—or a drunken doctor—or a drunken minister, over their door. The effect was such that the next day or two the publican had to take down the obnoxious sign, and thus some little good was done. The Highlander was not taught to associate himself with drunkenness—one of the stumbling blocks was removed out of his way.

As our readers are aware, Mr. Gough is not a man of commanding presence, no Hercules with portentous swagger, but a spare, meagre man of quiet manners, and gentle voice. He is not a man who takes one by storm, but one who grows on you, who finds his way to your heart and home so unsuspectingly, that you wonder how he ever managed to get there. His bodily presence is against him: he is a reed shaken by the wind, frail and feeble, and bowed down to the very dust till the afflatus comes, and he stands before you in the might and majesty of a presence and a power greater and grander than his own. Occasionally this want of manly appearance—for your popular orators are generally big burly men—is against him. A ludicrous instance of this occurred one night at a crowded meeting in New York, to which, as was rarely the case, for once, Mr. Gough was left to find his way alone. When he got to the chapel he found the aisles and every part full—it seemed impossible to gain admittance. Mr. Gough then tried the side doors, but with equally bad success. "Oh!" said a gentleman, "they will open;" but so dense was the crowd that in opening them a number of people were leaning against them fell to the ground, but still Mr. Gough was unable to effect an entrance. At first he managed to get along, till he came to a big broad-shouldered man, who would not move an inch, for all Mr. Gough could say to the contrary. The more Mr. Gough begged and prayed, the more resolutely he maintained his ground; he was a rock, and immovable as one. "Will you please to let me pass?" said Mr. Gough, timidly. "No," gruffly replied he, "that I shan't!" "I should like to get by you, sir, if you please," said Mr. Gough, in his mildest manner, "I have no doubt you would," said the other, in his sternest and bitterest and most sarcastic mood. "But my name is Gough, sir, and I have to lecture to-night," said Mr. Gough, as if that was a clencher, the effect of which he must feel. Mr. Gough might as well have attempted to fell a rhinoceros with feathers; the attempt produced quite the opposite effect to what was intended. The big man looked bigger and more athletic than ever, as he said, in a tone indicating that he was not to be taken in by Mr. Gough, or any one like him, "Now, young man, you can't come that game with me, I have let two or three Mr. Goughs go by already." Baffled as he was, Mr. Gough still insisted upon his identity, still maintained that he was the real Simon Pure, whatever impostors there might have been to the contrary, but all he could say was of no avail. "If you will let me pass the exercises will begin," said Mr. Gough overwhelmed with despair. His antagonist coolly surveyed him, took the measure of him from head to foot, and contemptuously replied, "You don't believe I am such a fool as to think that such a muff of a fellow as you could bring all these people together. Why you look so weak that I don't believe a quarter of them could hear you." Mr. Gough felt that his last chance was gone, and after some little parley gave it up. They say however when things are at the worst they mend. It was so in this case. Fortunately a lady was near who knew Mr. Gough, and seeing the difficulty he was in, asked him to cross over the top of her pew; but this was unnecessary. Mr. Gough's big antagonist gave way. Finding it was no use longer to be sceptical, he allowed the orator to pass, only adding in a grumbling tone, "If you are Mr. Gough begin as soon as you can, for I am tired of standing;" and it is hoped that when Mr. Gough once began his friend did not find he had been standing so long in vain.

It is a stale truth, but a truth nevertheless, that no

man can overrate the influence of woman. In this world of ours she is omnipotent—the highest and the lowest alike own her power—so true is it that—

> "Without the smile from partial beauty won,
> Oh, what were man! a world without a sun."

and, therefore, to get woman on his side—to enlist her sympathies and heart and action in his behalf—to teach her to believe in the truth and goodness of his cause, has been the aim of every reformer—social or moral—in these modern times. If this be true of England, it is still more true of America, where the larger scope of action given to woman adds to her advocacy a weight and influence that it is not supposed to possess here. As much as any man Mr. Gough has felt this and acted accordingly. Wherever he could do so, he has got woman to assist him in his glorious enterprise, and to her credit be it said, that to so great a work she has willingly given her noblest sympathies—her warmest prayers, and in many cases her very life. It was in the Apostles times the women who strengthened the hands and rejoiced the hearts of the teachers of truth, who but for them would have sunk beneath the burdens they were called to bear; and in our day it is the same. The cause must prosper which numbers amongst its advocates women, noble, self-denying, and pure. In America there are several ladies' colleges, and there have most of them been addressed by Mr. Gough, with a view to enlist the sympathies of the rising womanhood of the United States, and in most cases with singular success. Amongst the colleges thus visited, and with singular success, were the Wesley College, Cincinnati, the Pittsfield Institute, and the Stubenville Ladies'

Seminary. At Cincinnati, on one occasion, the ladies after he had visited them, invited him a second time for the purpose of gratifying him with a musical entertainment. In the course of it, one lady asked Mr. Gough to write in her album; very naturally he wrote the pledge for her. The other ladies hastened to follow the example; for three hours Mr. Gough was writing, till his hand ached, and he was obliged to give it up. One hundred and forty-three pledges were thus written. This led to other parties coming forward in a similar manner, and thus Mr. Gough, during his stay in Cincinnati wrote upwards of six hundred pledges. In the same manner he wrote pledges for hundreds of boys in small account books. But, to return to the ladies. One of the most pleasing effects in connexion with them was the formation of a Ladies' Association in Philadelphia— ladies' meetings had previously been held in some of the largest churches in the city—and when formed it numbered a thousand ladies as its members. This association was most active in its efforts for the promotion of the common cause. They employed a gentleman to attend the legislature one whole session to watch the proceedings, and to seek occasion of conferring with the legislators. They started a house of industry for the poor, which to this day is in a thriving condition, and got up a petition, signed by twenty thousand females, against granting licenses. All over the country their example was followed. At Buffalo one of the ladies connected with the association was the daughter of a gentleman afterwards President of the United States.

Equally important, also, Mr. Gough considered the young men of his adopted land—the youth, on whose future America hangs trembling for her fate. It has been his invariable aim to seize every opportunity of addressing them. At the Union College, Shenectady, he spoke, by invitation of the president, Dr. Nott, and two-thirds of the students, in the chapel immediately after the address signed the pledge. When he delivered an oration to the students of the National and State Law School, Ballston, more than half of them became abstainers, and one of them is now a popular advocate, and a professor in the same college. The Collegiate Institute at Poughkeepsie, Mr. Gough also visited with a similar result. Another college he visited was Williams's College —one of the oldest in the United States, but possessing this other speciality as well, viz., that every student is required to sign an agreement, promising to abstain from intoxicating drinks while he is at the college. The punishment for the violation of this law is for the first offence a reprimand; for the second expulsion, with no hope of being allowed to return. To this law the sons of the richest and the poorest were alike subject. Perhaps it would be as well were some similar law adopted at the more aristocratic universities at home. Gibbon tells us, that at Oxford he imbibed prejudice and port, and though we may suppose that in this enlightened age prejudices have long since ceased to visit that illustrious seat of learning, still it is notorious that the use of port has not been forgotten, and that the wine parties of Cambridge and Oxford are not always such as religious men could cordially approve. Even the medical students listened with attention to Mr. Gough. In America, as in England, they are generally considered rather a rough and unmanageable sect, when Mr. Gough however lectured to 800 of them, he was received by them with respect, and listened to—as he is always listened to—with interest and admiration and delight. Indeed it is patent in the United States that the young men, especially in the colleges, have always evinced the greatest disposition to hear Mr. Gough; and, consequently, he has seized every opportunity of addressing them in their chapels and public halls. At some he has lectured repeatedly; Yale College he has visited twice; Princeton twice; Amherst three times; Brunswick once; the University of Virginia once; Williams Town once; Dickenson; Carlisle once, and Brown University, Rhode Island. Some of the learned bodies have very properly conferred honours on Mr. Gough. The Eliosophic Literary Society of Princeton elected him one of their honorary members; other societies have done themselves honour in a similar way. But perhaps amongst no classes has Mr. Gough laboured with more delight than he has amongst children. We have already referred to his meetings amongst them. We may add here that Mr. Gough never stays a week in a place in America without gathering the children around him and addressing them. At Boston it is the custom to collect the children at the public schools together twice a year, and on such occasions Mr. Gough has repeatedly been invited to speak to them; and wherever he has gone he has done the same, and the little people have listened to him with delight, and have responded to him with enthusiasm. Many and many a little testimonial from them he treasures as amongst his dearest delights. At Cincinnati six fine little fellows waited on him as a deputation to present him with a gold pencil. At Gloucester six little girls came to him with book-marks. At Hartford a Bible was given to him with an inscription, purporting that it was presented to him by his little friends; but we need not extend our list. Mr. Gough has many such precious souvenirs; but the most cheering result of Mr. Gough's labours amongst them is not the testimonials he wins from them, or the enthusiasm he creates amongst them as he speaks; but the fact that he meets as young men and women those whom he knew a few years previous as children, in important mercantile positions, wielding influence and power in society, at the same time faithful to the principles Mr. Gough had infused into their youthful hearts.

Nor does Mr. Gough confine himself to these classes alone. He goes wherever he can, to preach temperance, to wean men from the most fatal of all vices, which, so long as it be continued in, shuts out its victim from happiness in this life, and hopes of happiness in that which is to come. For this purpose he has gone into the abodes of the criminal, and endeavoured to lead him back to virtue and to God. When Mr. Gough was in New York state, he spoke to the prisoners in the state prison, and so tender and touching and true were his words, that while he spoke almost all of them were in tears; and when asked if when out of prison they would abstain from drink, more than four-fifths of them held up their hands. At Auburn he went round the cells with their chaplains. One case particularly affected him. It was that of a young Englishman, in prison for forgery—a crime of which there was no doubt whatever that he was innocent. It seems that he was the son of a gentleman holding a highly respectable government appointment in England; that he had come to America with as much money as he required; that he had fallen into dissipated company, and that under the influence of drink he had got rid of his English sovereigns, and exchanged them for forged bank notes, which, not knowing them to be forged, he had put into circulation, and for the passing of which he had been unjustly condemned; but he was so stupified by drink at the time of the transaction, that he was unable to vindicate his innocence, and the penalty was, that he was thrown into jail; that he was wearing out when Mr. Gough visited him with unavailing shame and sorrow and regret. Mr. Gough never was more touched by any case. Auburn was not the only prison Mr. Gough visited. Besides, he went over the Massachusetts State Prison, Charlestown, Blackwells Island Penitentiary, Maryland Penitentiary, the Indiana State Prison, and that of New Hampshire. In all of these seed was sown which, it is trusted, will at some future day spring up and blow, and gladden men. Perhaps some of Mr. Gough's best meetings have been amongst the sailors; but as we have no particulars we can only allude to them here.

Our readers have now got up to the time when Mr. Gough was led to visit his native country. Once nothing seemed more improbable. Fortunately a way was made clear, and Mr. Gough once more trod the land of his birth. Since 1848 Mr. Gough had received repeated applications from the Scottish Temperance League, and the British Temperance Association, to come to this country; and at the same time that he felt there were difficulties in the way, he hoped a day would come when those difficulties would be removed. In the meanwhile he continued his labours in the land of his adoption. In 1851 Mr. F. W. Kellogg visited England, where he was cordially received by the London Temperance League. On his return in the following year he paid Mr. Gough a visit. Mr. Kellogg was most enthusiastic on the subject of his own tour. He had gone through the length and breadth of the land. He had seen everything *couleur de rose*. His heart had been lightened, and his hands strengthened, by his sojourn on the other side of the Atlantic, and he, in the most urgent manner, was commissioned by the London Temperance League to induce Mr. Gough to visit England. The latter said it was utterly impossible,—his engagements did not admit of it,—it was a thing not to be thought of for an instant. Mr. Kellogg was not to be discouraged, and renewed the attack; he continued battling the subject for hours. At length, more to get rid of Mr. Kellogg's importunity than with any expectation that the League would accede to his terms, Mr. Gough said that he had generally ten or twelve weeks in the summer for the purpose of resting and recruiting himself. For once he would spend them in visiting England, on condition that the London Temperance League should defray his own expenses and those of his wife, to England and back, allowing him also a week in which to visit Paris, and a week for his native village, and four weeks for the League. Mr. Gough, as he told a friend, supposed that this was a settler, and that he should never hear from the League again. He wrote, and Mr. Kellogg wrote, but Mr. Gough had no idea that the League would accede to his terms. To his surprise, he received a reply from the League complying with them, only stipulating for six weeks instead of four. Mr. Gough accordingly had nothing left him but to come. He left America on the 20th of July, intending to return by the 20th of October, and proposing if he failed on the first night, as he was fearful he should, to return by the very ship which brought him out. In doubt, and fear, and perplexity, he landed on our shores; but he was welcomed as a brother. At once he made his way to our hearts. At once he became at home. The 20th of October found Mr. Gough in England, where it is to be hoped we may find him for years to come.

We have said that the committee of the London Temperance League were the means of bringing Mr. Gough over to this country. It will not be out of place here if we attempt to chronicle the strenuous and unremitting efforts they made to ensure Mr. Gough's success. The remarkable results which had for several years followed the exertions of Mr. Gough as a temperance advocate in the United States, induced that committee to endeavour to have his valuable services extended to this country. As we have already said, Mr. Kellogg was the agent employed to induce Mr. Gough to comply with their request. As soon as it became known to the committee that that was the case, the committee left no stone unturned, and in season and out of season were most indefatigable in making the British public familiar with the life and labours of Mr. Gough. They felt their responsibility was great; that they had gone to some considerable expense; that if Mr. Gough's visit was a failure they would have to bear the blame, and they wisely resolved, that as far as they individually were concerned the very reverse should be the case. They determined to use every exertion to make Mr. Gough's visit memorable in the annals of the temperance cause. For this purpose a large number of copies of Mr. Gough's Autobiography, published as one of the Ipswich Tracts, was procured, and introduced to the notice of those attending the various May meetings in London. At the request of the committee, Mr. John Taylor kindly undertook to deliver, free of all expense, several lectures on "the Life and Mission of John B. Gough," by which means his coming visit was well advertised throughout the temperance ranks. A circular, including the Life of Mr. Gough, was also addressed to the various ministers of religion in London and its vicinity. These circulars were kindly attended to, and in many cases the visit of Mr. Gough was announced from the pulpit. Circulars of a similar tendency were also sent to most of the large employers of labour in the metropolis. Attention was also paid to the literary profession, every distinguished member of which received a special invitation, as did also the entire public press. To the provincial journals, as well as to those of the metropolis, Mr. Gough's Autobiography was sent, together with an abstract of his labours, which in many cases was inserted. An extensive system of advertising was also resorted to, and thus almost every newspaper was induced to spread the knowledge of the intended demonstration in every circle, whether high or low, rich or poor. Exeter Hall, and the large room of the Whittington Club, were engaged, and confident with joy and hope did the committee await the result.

At length July 31, 1853, came, and Mr. and Mrs. Gough arrived at Liverpool, where they were warmly received by Smith Harrison, Esq., a Liverpool merchant, and other gentlemen connected with that town. The electric telegraph conveyed the anxiously expected intelligence to London. At an early hour on Monday, August 1, the committee of the League, with other friends, assembled at the terminus of the North Western Railway. At a little past four the train from Liverpool arrived, and Mr. Gough was received with a brotherly welcome by his fellow-countrymen and fellow-labourers, who accompanied him to the house of George Cruikshank, Esq., where the *elite* of the temperance body had been invited, and had assembled to welcome the long-anticipated guest. On the following day, August 2, the first great meeting was held in Exeter Hall. It was a day on which much depended,—which the committee looked forward to with mingled hopes and fears,—and anxiously regarded by thousands in all parts of the land. It was the day which was to justify the committee, and to establish the reputation of Mr. Gough on English soil. As early as four o'clock P.M., persons were waiting to obtain admission to the Hall, though the time announced for opening the doors was six, and the proceedings did not commence till eight; and no sooner were the doors opened than every part commanding a view of the speaker was immediately filled. Never did that magnificent hall—that hall so famed for oratory, the effects of which have been felt in the uttermost parts of the earth,—so famed for its assemblies, which have comprised the noblest spirits of the age,—never, we repeat, did that magnificent hall present a nobler sight; the benches crowded with living souls showed how deep was the interest created by the speaker and his theme, whilst the banners of different nations, placed in various parts of the hall, showed how universal in its application was the temperance cause. On the platform, the national flags of England and America waved harmoniously together, as it is to be hoped they may do to the end of time. "It was a noble sight," an American said; "to see it would well repay a journey across the Atlantic." The united choirs of the Temperance singing societies of the metropolis, and the

Shapcott band, occupied the centre of the vast platform in front of the great organ, the use of which was kindly granted by the Sacred Harmonic Society. The excitement reached its height when Mr. Gough came on the platform, leaning on the arm of the President of the League, J. S. Buckingham, Esq., attended by the leaders of the temperance cause, gathered from every corner of the land. Description of the scene was impossible,—language fails. The enthusiasm was unbounded;—many wept for joy. At length it calmed down, and after a brief but appropriate address from the chairman, Mr. Gough for the first time spoke to an audience in his native land. He had left our shores a boy; he had come back to them a man. He had left unnoticed and unknown; he had come back with a world-wide fame. He had gone out poor; he had returned rich with the blessings of those he had saved from intemperance and sin. He had sunk into the lowest depths of despair, and he had repented and gathered strength, and was now rewarded with the approval of conscience, and in his heart the peace of God. It was a night of trial for him; yet he was equal to the task. Great as had been the expectations created, Mr. Gough surpassed them all. The vast multitude he swayed as if with an enchanter's wand. As he willed, it was moved to laughter or melted into tears. All doubt vanished:—it was felt that he had made good his reputation here,—that all that had been promised he had redeemed. We reprint an article which appeared in the *Weekly News* at the time, from the pen of Mr. J. Ewing Ritchie, giving an account of Mr. Gough's visit, as a proof of the effect produced on an impartial observer:—

"Excuse us, kind sir, if this week we have no scenes in the House to record—nothing to tell of Parliamentary business and dulness. A week of monotonous routine offers little for our pen, and is as wearisome a task for us to write as it must be for you to read. Excuse us, then, if we take you elsewhere—to one of those popular parliaments which are so common in our midst—the influence of which for good and bad, no legislator can overlook—to which often the assembly in Palace-yard is compelled to bow.

"On your right hand side as you pass along the Strand you see a lofty door, evidently leading to some immense building within. It is called Exeter Hall, for it stands where, in old times, stood Exeter Change, and still has its live lions, which are very numerous, especially in the months of May and June. You enter the door and ascend a long and ample staircase which conducts you to the finest public room in the metropolis. What popular passions have I not seen here! What contradictory utterances have I not heard here! High Church—Low Church—Methodism—Dissent—have all appealed from that platform to those benches crowded with living souls. From that platform, accompanying that organ, seven hundred voices join often in Handel's majestic strains. Underneath me are the offices of the various societies whose aim are among the noblest that can be proposed to man. Westminster Hall is a fine hall, but this in which I am is eight feet wider than that. 131 feet long, 76 feet wide, and 45 feet high, and will contain with comfort more than 3,000 persons. On the night of which I now write it was well filled by an audience, such as a few years back could not have been collected for love or money, but which now can be got together with the greatest ease, not merely in London, but in Manchester, in Birmingham, in Liverpool, in all our great seats of industry, of intelligence, and life. I mean an audience of men and women who have come to see intemperance to be the great curse of this our age and land, and who have resolved to abstain themselves from all intoxicating drink, and to encourage others to do so as well. Evidently something great was expected. The western gallery was covered with tastefully-decorated cloth, on which was inscribed in emblazoned silver letters, thirty inches deep, "The London Temperance League," with an elaborate painted border, composed of garlands of flowers. The Royal Gallery and the smaller one opposite, was covered with scarlet cloth, on which were arranged rose-coloured panels, with the words, 'London Temperance League,' in silver letters. The front of the platform and the reporters'-box was also decorated in a similar manner. At the end of the Royal Gallery was fixed a large royal standard, the folds of which hung gracefully over the heads of the audience. Under the royal standard was placed the union-jack. At the end of the opposite gallery proudly waved the banner of the great Republic of the West. The platform was decorated with flags, bearing inscriptions of various kinds. Like the stars in the heavens, or the sands on the sea shore, they were innumerable. In front of the organ were arranged the choir of the Temperance Societies, and on the floor of the platform were placed the Shapcott family, with their Sax-horns.

"Why was all this preparation made? For what purpose that living multitude of warm hearts? The answer is soon given. Some twenty-four years back a poor lad, without money and learning—almost without friends—was shipped off to America, to try his fortune in the New World. Arrived there, the lad became a man, lived by the sweat of his brow, learned to drink, to be a boon companion, and fell as most fall; for there is that in the flowing bowl and the wine when it is red, which few can withstand. Friends left him; he became an outcast and a wanderer; he sank lower and lower; he walked in rags, he loathed life; his frame became emaciated with disease; there was none to pity or to save. It seemed for that man there was nothing left but to lie down and die. However, whilst there is life there is hope. That man, in his degradation and despair was reached; he signed the Temperance pledge, he became an advocate of the Temperance cause. His words were words of power; they touched men's hearts, they fired men's souls; he led the life of an apostle; wherever he went the drunkard was reclaimed; zeal was excited, the spell of the sparkling cup was gone, humanity was saved, and now he had returned for a while to his native land to advocate the cause which had been a salvation to his own soul and life, and these men and women — these hopeful youths — these tender-hearted maidens—had come to give him welcome. Already every eye in that vast assembly is turned to the quarter whence it is expected the hero of the night will appear. At length the appointed hour arrives, a band of Temperance reformers move towards the platform with the flags of Britain and America waving, as we trust they may long do, harmoniously together—we see familiar faces—Cruikshank—Buckingham—Cassell—but there is one form we know not, it is that of a stranger, it is that of Gough. A few words from Mr. Buckingham, who presides, and the stranger comes forward, but he is no stranger, for the British greeting, that almost deafens his ears, while it opens his heart, makes him feel himself at once at home.

"Well, popular enthusiasm has toned down—the audience has reseated itself—a song of welcome has been sung, and there stands up a man of middle size, and middle age. Lord Bacon deemed himself ancient when he was thirty-one—we moderns, in our excessive self-love, delude each other into the belief that we are middle-aged when we are anywhere between forty and sixty. In reality, a middle-aged man should be somewhere about thirty-five, and such we take to be Mr. Gough's age. He is dressed in sober black—his hair is dark, and so is his face; but there is a muscular vigour in his frame, for which we were not prepared. We should judge Gough has a large share of the true *elixir vitæ*—animal spirits. His voice is one of great power and pathos, and he speaks without an effort. The first sentence as it falls gently and easily from his lips, tells us that Gough has that true oratorical power which neither money nor industry, nor persevering study, can ever win. Like the poet, the orator must be born. You may take a man six feet high—he shall be good-looking—have a good voice, and speak English with a correct pronunciation—you shall write for that man a splendid speech—you shall have him taught elocution by Mr. Webster, and yet you shall no more make that man an orator than, to use a homely phrase, you can make a silk purse out of a sow's ear. Gough is an orator born. Pope tells us he 'lisped in numbers,' and in his boyhood Gough must have had the true tones of the orator on his tongue. There was no effort—no fluster—all was easy and natural. He was speaking for the first time, to a public meeting in his native land—speaking to thousands who had come with the highest expectations —who expected much and required much—speaking, by means of the press, to the whole British public. Under such circumstances, occasional nervousness would have been pardonable; but, from the first, Gough was perfectly self-possessed. There are some men who have prodigious advantages on account of appearance alone. We think it was Fox who said it was impossible for any one to be as wise as Thurlow looked. The great Lord Chatham was particularly favoured by nature in this respect. In our own time—in the case of Lord Denman —we have seen how much can be done by means of a portly presence and a stately air. Gough has nothing of this. He is just as plain a personage as George Dawson, of Birmingham would be, if he were to cut his hair and shave off his moustache; but, though we have named George Dawson, Gough does not speak like him, or any other living man. Gough is no servile copy, but a real original. We have no one in England we can compare him to. Our popular lecturers, such as George Dawson, Henry Vincent, George Thompson, are very different men. They have all a studied quaintness or a studied rhetoric. There is something artificial about them all. In Gough there is nothing of this. He seems to speak by inspiration. As the apostles spoke who were commanded not to think beforehand what they should say—the spoken word seems to come naturally, as air-bubbles up from the bottom of the well. In what he said there was nothing new—there could be nothing new—the tale he told was old as the hills, yet, as he spoke an immense audience grew hushed and still, and hearts were melted, and tears glistened in female eyes, and that great human mass became knit together by a common spell. Disraeli says, Sir Robert Peel played upon the House of Commons as an old fiddle; Gough did the same at Exeter Hall. At his bidding, stern, strong men, as well as sensitive women, wept or laughed —they swelled with indignation or desire. Of the various chords of human passion, he was master. At times he became roused, and we thought how

————— 'in his ire Olympian Pericles
Thundered and lightened, and all Hellas shook.'

"At other times in his delineation of American manners, he proved himself almost an equal to Selsbee. Off the stage we have nowhere seen a better mimic than Gough, and this must give him great power, especially in circles where the stage is much a *terra incognita* as Utopia, or the Island of Laputa itself. We have always thought that a fine figure of Byron, where he tells us that he laid his hand upon the ocean's mane. Something of the same kind might be said to be applicable to Mr. Gough. He seemed to ride upon the audience—to have mastered it completely to his will. He seemed to bestride it as we could imagine Alexander bestriding his Bucephalus.

"Gough spoke for nearly two hours. Evidently the audience could have listened, had he gone on, till midnight. We often hear that the age of oratory has gone by—that the press supersedes the tongue—that the appeal must henceforth be made to the reader in his study, not to the hearer in the crowded hall. There is much truth in that. Nevertheless the true orator will always please his audience, and true oratory will never die. The world will always respond to it. The human heart will always leap up to it. The finest efforts of the orator have been amongst civilized audiences. It was a cultivated audience before whom Demosthenes pleaded; to whom, standing on Mars-hill, Paul preached of an unknown God. The true orator, like the true poet, speaks to all. He gathers around him earth's proudest as well as poorest intellects. Notwithstanding, then, the march of mind, oratory may win her triumphs still. So long as the heart is true to its old instinct—so long as it can pity, or love, or hate, or fear, it will be moved by the orator, if he can but pity or love, or hate or fear himself. This is the true secret. This is it that made Gough the giant that he is. Without that he might be polished, learned, master of all human lore; but he would be feeble and impotent as the—

'Lorn lyre that ne'er hath spoken
Since the sad day its master chord was broken.'"

It was the same when Mr. Gough visited Scotland. It was said he would do for England, but not for the coldly critical audiences of the modern Athens. There, however, as here, Mr. Gough found the way to all hearts, roused a similar enthusiasm, and achieved a similar success. It was calculated, that by the close of the year Mr. Gough had addressed no fewer than 104,600 persons, and that not fewer than 3,000 had taken the pledge in consequence of his addresses. In his first visit to London alone he had spoken to 30,000. Perhaps one of the most memorable meetings in connexion with Mr. Gough in England, was that held in St. Martin's Hall on the evening of December 28, 1853, when children to the number of 1,000, belonging to the Bands of Hope, were present, and when, at the request of the committee, the Earl of Shaftesbury presided. At the conclusion of Mr. Gough's address, in acknowledging a vote of thanks, his lordship said, "I do not think thanks are due to me for sitting here and listening to the most eloquent, touching, convincing and effective address I have ever heard, or was ever delivered on any other platform; and I am sure you will join with me in thanking Mr. Gough, which I heartily do, for his efforts; and I thank God who has brought him to this country, as I trust, to do a great work; and I am sure you will promise with me, to do as the children in America have done—help him to the best of our ability. The longer I live the more I am convinced that intemperance is the cause of a very large amount of national evils, both at home and abroad; and unless it is obstructed in its onward march, it will in this country, as in Australia, prove ruinous to society. I feel also convinced, that the future destinies of this great country are in the hands of such as those who form the majority of the present interesting meeting, and it will be by their instrumentality that those evils over which we mourn will be ultimately removed. I again say, that the future destinies of this land, my young friends, are in your hands, and I would therefore exhort you to continue combating with those evils which have been so eloquently placed before you this evening by our friend Mr. Gough. We must have by-and-by a new generation of men and women, and I may say, that such men as Mr. Gough, and I may also name Mr. Smithies, the editor of that excellent little paper addressed to the Bands of Hope,—are doing much towards bringing about that state of things which will transpire when those of us who have passed the meridian of life shall have ceased our labours to better the condition of society."

From London Mr. Gough has found his way into all our crowded homes of busy life. He has travelled over almost all England and Scotland. The chief towns of each county he has repeatedly visited, and wherever he has gone he has received but one kind of welcome, and his visits have led but to one result. It has been felt that Mr. Gough has opened a way for the propagation of temperance principles in circles where those principles had been viewed with indifference, contempt or disdain. Amongst his auditory have been such ladies as the Duchess of Sutherland,—amongst his chairmen such noblemen as the Earl of Shaftesbury and Lord Robert Grosvenor. Many members of our senate,—many of our most popular divines—many of our ablest writers—have listened to his addresses, and thus the influence of temperance principles have been extended far and wide. As regards the temperance cause itself, equally gratifying has been the result. Mr. Gough's advent has revived the energy of the temperance ranks. The good old cause is again dear,—the old love is again felt,—the old cry is again heard,—the old fire is again seen. The old banner again floats in triumph, and complete success seems near at hand!

To Mr. Gough himself his tour in his native land must have afforded peculiar pleasure. Some of the incidents connected with it must have been peculiarly grateful to a mind sensitive as his own. For instance, on the anniversary of his birth-day, August 24, 1854, a meeting was got up by the Temperance Association of the romantic little village in which Mr. Gough was born. It was a memorable day for Sandgate. In the afternoon addresses were delivered by Messrs. Geary,

M'Curry, Campbell, White, and Tweedie, of the committee of the London Temperance League to the children of Sandgate and the immediate neighbourhood, who had assembled for that purpose in considerable numbers; and at the close each child received from Mr. Gough a copy of his address to the Bands of Hope in St. Martin's Hall. In the evening a public meeting was held in the National School-room, which had been kindly lent for that purpose by the clergyman of the parish, and at which that able artist and zealous teetotaler, George Cruikshank, Esq., presided. To a meeting crowded in every part Mr. Gough delivered one of his most effective addresses. The occasion was affecting. It was his birthday. Thirty-seven years before he was a babe. The lonely hut in which he was born was yet standing; those who knew his beloved mother,—those who knew him as a poor soldier's boy, were around him. He had travelled far from his early home : he had dwelt amidst the men and cities of the far distant West. He had wandered in the ways of sin far from peace and happiness and God. He had been steeped to the very lips in poverty and misery, and degradation and shame,—and yet he had been saved as a brand from the burning. He had been led back to the narrow way from which he had so long strayed— and saved himself. He had been enabled to devote to the salvation of others a zeal that never tired; an eloquence that never wearied ; a tongue that never grew cold or dull. At the age of twelve he had gone forth from that village home—another twelve years and he had signed the temperance pledge—another twelve and he was back in his village home again. And here he was with beauty and fashion and wealth around; filling bright eyes with tears,—softening manly hearts,

—teaching the drunkard to burst his chains,—or showing the young how alone they could be safe. No wonder that the scene was one which will not be soon forgotten by those who were there; or that on Mr. Gough himself the effect was great, or that even in his strange career he could find no incident more startling or strange. And yet such passages are numerous in Mr. Gough's history.

The writer will not soon forget almost a similar one which happened in Drury Lane, in December, 1854. Old Drury was filled with as choice an audience as ever gathered within its capacious walls, for Mr. Gough was to give an address, and the Earl of Shaftesbury was to take the chair. It is unnecessary to add that Mr. Gough kept up the attention of his audience to the very last; that whether he were grave or gay—whether he told the old sad story, or called up smiles in all faces—his efforts were equally powerful. So much so, indeed, that the Earl of Shaftesbury, in returning thanks for his conduct in the chair, perhaps pronounced the most flattering, yet truthful, eulogiums which has ever greeted Mr. Gough. The Noble Earl referred in language perfectly unpremeditated, yet graceful and expressive, to the delight he had received from being permitted to listen to such addresses as those of Mr. Gough. He declared that it was utterly impossible to overrate the value of Mr. Gough's labours—that they were above all praise; and that he deemed the preservation of Mr. Gough's health, and his continuance in his advocacy of the temperance principles, as essential to the welfare, not of England or America alone, but of the whole civilized world. Such an allusion to himself in such a place, and from such a man—one of the very flower of our aristocracy, was too much for Mr. Gough. The past all came back to him again—all its pain and agony and despair. He thought of what he had been in that fearful time, and then he thought of what he was—of the peace and sunshine of the present, and again he rose to utter feelings which he could not repress—to say how bitter had been his path—what light and hope beamed on it now, and to record his entire consecration to the cause that had done so much for him. We need not add that the scene highly affected all present. 'What a sublime man it is!' said Soyer, the great *gastronome*, to the writer, as they came out of the theatre together. The writer felt that this was, perhaps, the highest compliment ever paid Mr. Gough. Soyer enthusiastic at a teetotal lecture, was a sight certainly we never expected to see.

And now we lay down the pen—our task is over. We have endeavoured to perform what we promised. Much more might be said—undoubtedly much remains to be told. Possibly our narrative, the critic may deem, unsatisfactory, but we have done our best, and if we but succeed in rivetting attention to Mr. Gough, and Mr. Gough's theme, we shall have done all at which we aimed. Mr. Gough is still in our midst, we can, therefore, say no more of him, but in taking leave of our subject, we cannot but express our hope that Mr. Gough's feeble strength may be renewed, that his residence among us may be continued, and that for many a coming year he may preach temperance—and what follows in its train—in his native land.

POETRY.

TWO YEARS AGO.

[Written for J. B. Gough.]

BY THE REV. JOHN PIERPONT.

Tune—'O no, we never mention him.'

Two years ago, a mighty chain
  Had bound me to the bowl,
Its links lay burning on my brain
  And crushing down my soul ;
My mother, far from scenes of strife
  Was, in her grave, laid low,
And not a star shone on my life
  But two short years ago.

Two years ago, the loafing throng,
  That hung around the inn,
Would say—'Come, sing us now a song,
  And you shall have some gin.'
And I the drunkard's catch would troll,
  The lowest of the low,
And then in drink would drown my soul,
  But two short years ago.

Two years ago, upon the edge
  Of Ruin's gulf I lay :
I woke—I rose—I signed the pledge
  Two years ago to-day :

That pledge hath saved my drowning soul,
  From sorrow, pain, and woe;
'Twas that, that helped me dash the bowl
  Away, two years ago.

And now a glorious sun hath risen
  To cheer and bless my soul:
I feel my freedom from my prison—
  My bondage to the bowl.
A thousand friends, with anxious care,
  Their arms around me throw,
To keep me from the gulf of Fear
  I sought, two years ago.

Two years ago, thy name, O God,
  I named but to blaspheme;
Thy holy courts I never trod;—
  Forgive me, Power Supreme!
And help me do some little good,
  In lifting up the low,
Who now are standing, where I stood
  But two short years ago.

SONG.

Written by the Rev. WM. B. TAPPAN, for Mr. J. B. GOUGH, and sung by him at the Anniversary Occasion, October 28, 1844.

I WAS tossed by the winds on a treacherous wave;
Above me was peril, beneath me a grave;
The sky, to my earnest enquiry, was dark;
The storm in a deluge came down on my bark!
How fearful! to drive on a horrible shore,
Where breakers of Ruin eternally roar.

O, Mercy! to wreck in the morning of days,—
To die when life dazzles with changeable rays,—
To sink as the grovelling and vile of the ship,
The rose on my cheek, and the dew on my lip—
And fling, as a bauble, my soul to the heaps,
That glisten and mock from the caves of the deeps.

O, no! for a STAR trembles out in the sky,
The shrieks of the ocean complainingly die,
The gales that I covet blow fresh from the shore,
Where breakers of Ruin eternally roar:
Each sail presses homeward—all praises to THEE,
Whose word in that hour hushed tempest and sea!

TO J. B. GOUGH.

YOUNG champion of a righteous cause, press boldly on, I pray,
Though weary, faint not—falter not, though dark and rough the way;
Ripe is the harvest, and thy hand can well the sickle wield,
O! bind the sheaves—root up the tares, that cumber now the field.

Strong is the foe; but thou art strong, the tempter's spell to break;
Thy heel can bruise the serpent's head, his dreaming victim wake.
Still pour, in floods of burning light, thy thoughts without control.
Thy trumpet tones can stir the heart, can rouse the slumbering soul.

Sheathe not the two-edged sword of truth, till error vanquished lies;
Spare not the wolf, while yet one lamb, bleeding, before thee dies.
Ay, thine's a work of emprise high, a sweet reward is thine;
Enrolled 'mong blest philanthropists, thy name shall brightly shine.

Though, like the lightning-riven oak, thou'st known misfortune's storm,
Affections shall spring up, and twine, like ivy, round thy form.
Thousands shall grasp thy hand, and call thee saviour, brother, friend;
And prayers from myriad hearts for thee, like incense, shall ascend.

The seeds thou'rt sowing now in tears, shall blossom 'neath thy tread;
Hope's ripened fruits, and sole-fraught joys, shall cluster round thy head;
Angels of holy light o'er thee, their radiant wings shall bend,
With pæans of a rescued host, their harpings soft shall blend.

More precious to a soul like thine, such treasures, though untold,
Than ingots of the glistening dross that mammon's sons call gold.
Blessed thus on earth, a brighter crown shall deck thy brow above,
Where thou, with all earth's ransomed tribes, shall sing the song of love.

LIZETTE.

Dedham, Mill Village.

LINES

Suggested by hearing Mr. J. B. GOUGH, at a late Temperance Lecture, pourtray in glowing colours, the evils of Intemperance.

DAYS of my childhood,—sweet days of delight,—
When I thought that the world would thus ever be bright;
When the eyes of fond parents would light up with joy,
When they rested on me, their then innocent boy,—
  I dreamed not of sorrow,—I dreamed not of woe,—
  A long time ago, a long time ago.

I roamed with my sister, o'er highland and wood ;
And blithe was our song, from hearts happy and good ;
We culled the wild flower, fresh chaplets to twine,
To deck her fair brow, as she also did mine,—
  It seemed then a paradise, to us below,—
  A long time ago, a long time ago.

But those days of delight, ah ! they did not remain ;
For soon they were followed by want, and by pain ;
The mother, that loved me, in death passed away,
And I wept on the sod o'er her slumbering clay ;
  My sister and I stood where she lay low,—
  A long time ago, a long time ago.

We returned to our garret, so dreary and sad,
And felt that we never again could be glad ;
We knelt there in prayer to our heavenly Friend !
For, on earth, none was near us, to guard and defend !
  'Twas then that I first felt life's troubles and woe,—
  A long time ago, a long time ago.

My home was with strangers,—a poor orphan boy ;—
Then for ever was passed my childhood's bright joy,—
Rough language, ill treatment, ah ! hard was my lot ;
Such cruel unkindness can ne'er be forgot ;
  My efforts to please were returned with a blow,—
  A long time ago, a long time ago.

Then alone in the barn I have oft raised a prayer,
Unto him who extends to the ravens his care,
And thus sought for strength my hard lot to endure,
An unfriended orphan boy, tempted and poor ;
  For e'en then I could feel sin was bringing me low,—
  A long time ago, a long time ago.

My home, alas ! 'twas no home unto me ;
No smile from loved parents, no kind sympathy ;
So I sought when despondent, and lonely, and sad,
Some youthful companions, the jovial and glad ;
  They first gave the sweet poison,—I could not say, no,—
  A long time ago, a long time ago.

My home and my griefs were forgotten by me,
In the sweet poisoned draught I sought pleasure and glee;
I then was the happiest, merriest lad,
The world seemed so bright, and my heart seemed so glad;
   I thought it a friend, but found it a foe,—
   A long time ago, a long time ago.

These feverish dreams did but shortly remain,
And then followed remorse, contrition, and pain;
I tried to reform, but I only grew worse;—
O why did I taste of the poison at first!
   But no friend was near, kind advice to bestow,—
   A long time ago, a long time ago.

Years passed, and the youth is transformed to the man;
For a time I succeeded my sin to withstand,
I bid all my bottle-companions adieu,
For now other scenes had attracted my view,—
   A fair, gentle maiden, she loved me, I know—
   A long time ago, a long time ago.

A husband and father! O sad is the sight,
When these hallowed affections should meet with a blight!
My wife! how I loved her, no language can tell,
And yet from my promises sadly I fell!
   I, a husband and drunkard? ah, yes! it was so;—
   A long time ago, a long time ago.

Over years I would now cast oblivion's veil,
If not by recalling, I hope to prevail
On some tempted youth the first step to beware,
The many allurements that 's spread to ensnare;
   Much grief it would have saved me if I had said, no,—
   A long time ago, a long time ago.

Life is so changing, we cannot remain
One year to another exactly the same;
If the course is e'en downward, O! rapid the fall;
The path of the drunkard is warning to all;
   But no voice was then raised to warn me of woe;—
   A long time ago, a long time ago.

No voice! ah, yes! one gentle voice I did hear,
Who gave her advice with a sigh and a tear;
The wife of a drunkard! O hard was her task;
But neglect, grief, and suffering, relieved her at last.
  My wife and my babe death removed from below;—
  A long time ago, a long time ago.

When the day had been passed in revelry, glee,
And at night no home offered protection to me;
I would crawl to the churchyard, the moon shining bright,
And sit on the grave of my wife the lone night!
  Not a friend had I then in the wide world below!—
  A long time ago, a long time ago.

But the drama of life is now changéd again,
And I stand up the freeman,—I've broken my chain;
Ye friends of the outcast, who snatched me from death,
In thanks for my rescue I now raise my breath.
  O! I wish that my heart years since felt as now,—
  A long time ago, a long time ago.

Ye throngs, who are pressing to hear me repeat
My life's sad experience, O let me entreat,
'Touch not! O taste not! the danger is great;
Beware of the tempter before 'tis too late!
  I speak from a heart that its ills well did know,—
  A long time ago, a long time ago.

And thou, who for gain can extend to another
The poisonous cup! it is to thy brother,
That thou art dispensing this misery, pain;
He is a great loser! but small is thy gain;
  For the book of the prophet* revealed thine own woe,—
  A long time ago, a long time ago.

M. R.

* Habakkuk ii. 15.

DRINKING SONG.

DRINK from the mountain spring,
   As it leaps from its rocky cell;
Drink from the pure stream, wandering
   Along the flowery dell.

But drink not of the poisoned cup,
   Taste not its deadly flow;
It crazes the head, it fires the blood,
   And it fills the heart with woe.

Though it dance to the sight, in youth so bright,
   Though it gleam with the promise of joy,
Yet of Genius and Hope 't is the deadly blight,
And it cloudeth the morning of youth in night,
And it bringeth long woe for a brief delight,
   And it charmeth to destroy.

Then drink from the mountain spring,
   As it leaps from its rocky cell;
Drink from the pure stream, wandering
   Along the flowery dell.

But drink not of the poisoned cup,
   O! taste not its deadly flow,
For it crazes the head, and it fires the blood,
   And it fills the heart with woe.

                                          J. P.

New Brunswick, 1845.

ORATIONS,

BY

JOHN B. GOUGH.

www.ingramcontent.com/pod-product-compliance
Lightning Source LLC
LaVergne TN
LVHW061214060426
835507LV00016B/1933